RUN!

26.2 STORIES OF BLISTERS AND BLISS

DEAN KARNAZES

ALLEN&UNWIN

First published in Great Britain in 2011

This paperback edition published in 2012

Allen & Unwin
c/o Atlantic Books
Ormond House
26–27 Boswell Street
London WC1N 3JZ
Phone: 020 7269 1610
Fax: 020 7430 0916
Email: uk@allenandunwin.com
Web: www.atlantic-books.co.uk

Allen & Unwin
83 Alexander Street
Crows Nest NSW 2065
Australia
Phone: (61 2) 8425 0100
Fax: (61 2) 9906 2218
Email: info@allenandunwin.com
Web: www.allenandunwin.com

A CIP catalogue record for this book is available from the British Library.

ISBN 978 1 74237 793 3

Printed in Great Britain by Clays Ltd, St Ives plc

10 9 8 7 6 5 4 3 2 1

To my lovely wife, Julie, thank you for faithfully putting up with me for all these years. We've had some fun, and we're not done yet!

Contents

Prerun Stretch ix
Warmup xi

1.0 When All Else Fails, Start Running..........................1

2.0 Follow Dreams, Not Rules............................15

3.0 Are You High?.......................................25

4.0 The Reunion..29

5.0 It Only Hurts When I Run..........................37

6.0 Running in the Dark—Naked.......................43

7.0 Passing the Buck..................................67

8.0 Never Say Never...................................71

9.0 Seconds Matter....................................83

10.0 Run for the Hills................................91

11.0 Dreadville......................................101

12.0 Get After It....................................113

13.0 What's Your Scene?.............................125

14.0 Living with an Athlete.........................131

15.0 First Is Best...................................139

16.0 4 Deserts and Some Badwater.............................155

17.0 Atacama Aftermath..167

18.0 My Toughest Ultra...175

19.0 Hotter Than Yesterday...179

20.0 Letters to Karno...187

21.0 Sahara Sirens...197

22.0 The Best Race of My Life....................................205

23.0 SOS..209

24.0 Forty-Eight Hours of Chafing............................217

25.0 Shark Bait...237

26.0 Onward and Upward..245

26.2 There Is No Finish Line.......................................255

Afterword: A Run Across America 257
Cool Down 271
About the Author 273

Prerun Stretch

RUN! is comprised of 26.2 short stories about running and about life. Why 26.2, you may ask? As you probably know, there are 26.2 miles in a marathon. Each story in this book is distinct and stands on its own, just as each mile of a marathon has its own unique personality. Together, the 26.2 miles of a marathon tell a complete story, just as the chapters of this book will coalesce to form a complete tale, one of blisters and bliss. But unlike a real marathon, this isn't going to hurt as much. So enjoy every step of the way!

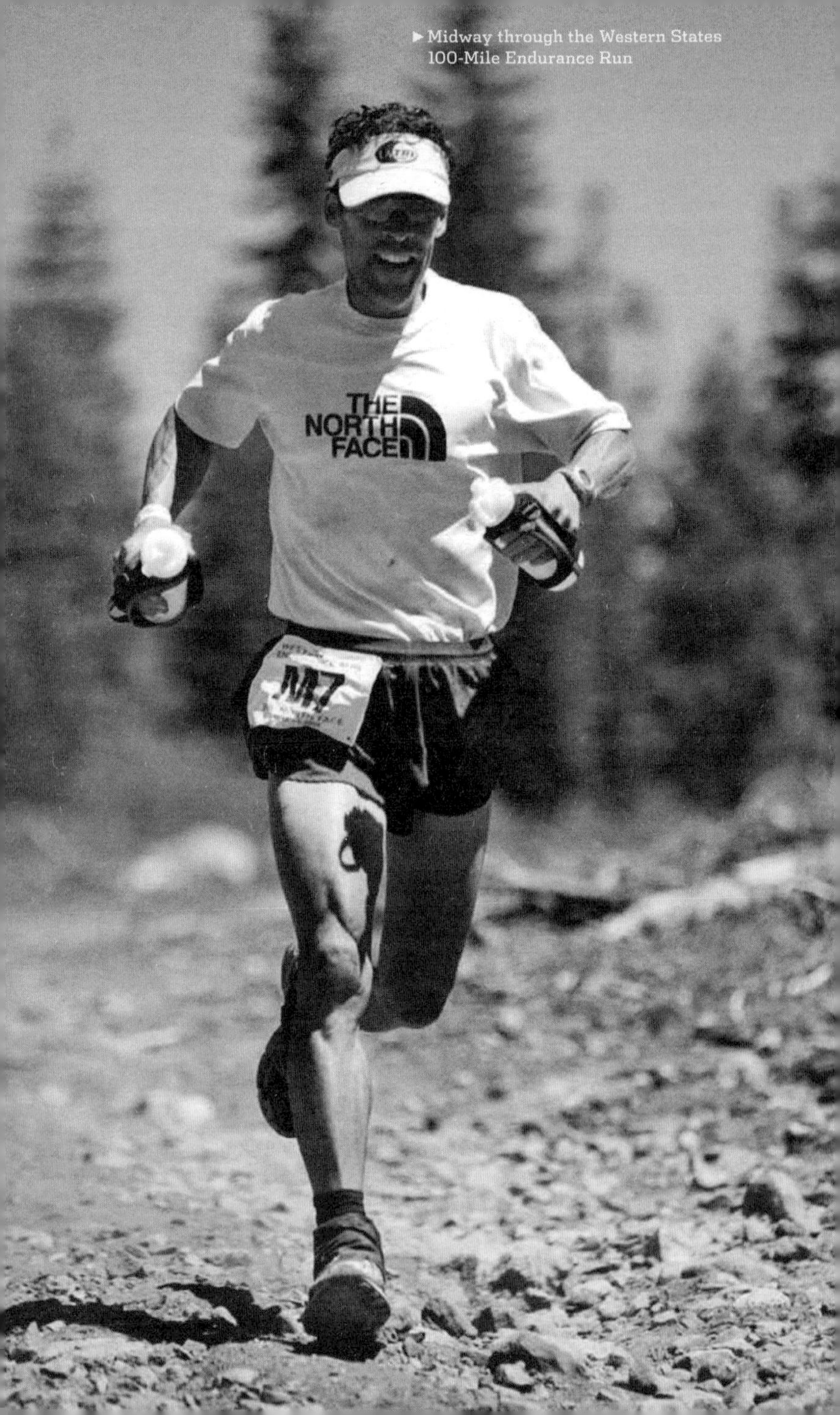

▶ Midway through the Western States 100-Mile Endurance Run

Warmup

"When you pray, move your feet."
—OLD AFRICAN PROVERB

THE HUMAN BODY was made to move. Everything about us was designed for locomotion, engineered for movement. Our modern world, however, invites just the opposite: idleness.

We go from our air-conditioned cars to the elevators of our climate-controlled buildings to our comfortable office chairs. Modern rationale equates comfort and convenience—the total absence of pain and struggle—with happiness. I, along with a growing number of like-minded individuals, think that just the opposite may be true. We've grown so comfortable, we're miserable.

Personally, I never feel more alive than when I'm in great pain, struggling to persevere against insurmountable odds and untold adversity. Hardship? Suffering? Bring it! I've said it before and I've come to believe it: There's magic in misery.

I realize this notion runs contrary to the pervasive modern day sentiment. Some people will understand this mind-set; others will not. Returning from my daily run the other morning, I came upon my neighbor, out in his slippers collecting the morning paper. He looked at me in my running gear and asked, "Doesn't running hurt?" I thought about his question briefly. "It does if you're doing it right," I said. He gazed at me quizzically, trying to make sense of a comment that seemed counterintuitive. Like I said, some people get this way of thinking, others don't.

Regardless of your slant, I hope you enjoy what you are about to read. Unlike most books by athletes, I wrote every word of this book myself . . . er, *spoke* every word of it myself. You see, in accordance with the premise of being built for movement, I "wrote" much of this book largely by dictating into the digital recorder on my smart phone while running. No sitting on my butt in front of a static computer here. This book was composed "on the run."

My hope is that my true voice comes through. If nothing else, know that each passage was constructed with great pain, sweat, and struggle. As you might expect, I wouldn't want it any other way.

When All Else Fails, Start Running

"Now you wouldn't believe me if I told you, but I could run like the
wind blows. From that day on, if I was ever going somewhere,
I was running!"

—FORREST GUMP

HOOD TO COAST is a 197-mile twelve-person relay race.
Why I was running it solo was for one reason and one reason only:
Adventure!

Dear ol' Mom and Dad were also along for the ride, as was tradition. They'd joined me as my crew, supporting me on many such escapades. In fact, they looked forward to these outings as much as I did: the places we'd go, the people we'd meet along the way, the encounters we'd have—it was all an exciting journey into the unknown.

Last night, during the first night of all-night running, we'd passed by a house in the countryside only to be spotted by the owner

who invited us in for some freshly picked berry pie. She was delight-
ful and the pie was otherworldly delicious. It was after midnight.

Now, some twenty-four hours later, Mom lay strewn across the
passenger seat of the crew vehicle, snoozing. After nearly two days
of continuous running, I was feeling a bit groggy myself. Much to
my delight, we came upon a twenty-four-hour convenience store. I
desperately needed coffee and made a dash for the door. Dad always
carried the cash since I was clad in running gear, so I was glad to see
him pull in after me.

The gentleman behind the counter eyed us with suspicion, perhaps judging us against the height marks on the entrance doors that
convenience stores use to ID criminals. We were the only people in
the store. I immediately darted for the self-serve coffee section to
prepare a cup of brew. My dad ambled toward the checkout register.

Along with the coffee, there were various flavored creamers.
They had vanilla, hazelnut, chocolate mint, and a host of other
delectable choices. I began concocting the ultimate cup of convenience store brew. My dad and the checkout clerk watched as I care-
fully crafted my little cup of paradise. Finally, Dad turned to the
man and said, "He's been running for two days now. He started up
at Mount Hood." The clerk didn't respond.

"He's trying to get to the coast," Dad went on. The clerk kept
his eyes transfixed on me.

"Doing it to celebrate his 40th birthday. It will take him about
forty-five hours," my dad continued.

That did it; enough was enough. "Go on, take your coffee!" the
clerk barked. "Have it. That's fine. Just go!"

His sharp words sent my dad and me reeling. It took a moment to
compute, but then I realized what was going on here. He thought we

were beggars. I could imagine his mind working: A young guy comes in and pours himself a presumptive cup of coffee, stalling so that the old guy can deliver a fancifully inventive pitch to get the goods for free.

My dad recognized the clerk's misunderstanding as well. "Oh no," he said, "I was just telling you this to let you know, that's all."

"Go!" the man continued. "Get out! Take your coffee and leave."

"Look," my dad said, pulling a five-dollar bill out of his pocket, "we had every intention of paying you."

The man shouted at us, pointing at the door. "I do not want your money! Just take your coffee and get out!"

I realized now where the breakdown in communication had arisen. Beyond the clear cultural differences, the misunderstanding was heightened by the fact that it was 3:00 A.M. and by my strange outfit, one he'd probably never seen before in the store, if ever. (I wore a brightly colored singlet, shorts, reflective ankle bracelets, clear glasses, and a headlamp.) Add on top of all this some old loon claiming that his young accomplice was running hundreds of miles for days on end without rest, and the setup was all too obvious. The clerk would not be played for a fool; he knew better!

It was an honest mistake, one I was willing to leave at that. So I started toward the exit with my coffee.

"Son," my dad instructed me, "put the coffee back."

"What? Are you kidding?"

"Son, put the coffee back. He won't take our money. Let's go."

"Look, with all due respect, Pops, there is absolutely zero possibility I'm gonna put this coffee back. He said I could have it."

My father stomped over to me and got right up in my face. "Son, put the coffee down!"

I started to raise the cup to my mouth, and he grabbed my arm, forcing it down. We began to struggle, and I started to think this would be the first time ever my dad and I got into a fistfight. I didn't care. I wanted my coffee!

"Take it outside, you two!" the clerk yelled. "Just leave or I'll call the cops!"

My father turned back to face the man. In that brief instant, I managed to take a gulp of the hot brew. It scalded my mouth, and I cried out.

My dad glared at the clerk. From behind his back I gestured frantically to the clerk with both arms for him to continue elaborating. I needed him to distract my dad for as long as possible so that I could take another sip.

Unfortunately, my dad saw the reflection of what I was doing in the window. He whirled around to me. "Son," he commanded, "put down the coffee!"

It was obvious this was going nowhere. In somber retreat, I put the coffee back on the counter and walked out the door, head slung low. My dad eventually followed.

We reconnected on the sidewalk. "That was crazy," I said. Trying to make light of the situation, I went on, "At least I got a sip of coffee for free."

"It wasn't free. I left the money inside," my dad proclaimed with defiant pride.

"What?"

"I left the money on the counter."

"You put that five-dollar bill on the counter?" I asked in disbelief. "Did he take it?"

"No, the ungrateful buffoon. He just brushed it to the floor with the back of his hand and said, 'Your money is no good here.' "

"So where's the money now?"

"It's sitting in a wad on the floor."

I turned around and started walking back inside.

"Where are you going?" my dad asked.

"I'm going back in there to get my coffee."

"Oh no you don't!" He ran over and jumped in front of me. He put his hands out in front of his chest like an offensive lineman, preparing to prevent my reentering into the store.

"But we paid for it." He didn't budge.

I shook my head in saddened defeat. My dad and the clerk weren't all that different. These men, with their old-world ways, were so proud, there was no use trying to argue with them. Stubborn pride was just part of their hard-wiring. Precious stuff, actually, for it provided the fodder that turned a rather surly interaction into an endearing lifelong memory, one that my parents and I would cherish for years to come.

• • • •

Flash forward the better part of a decade and things have changed a bit. My parents and I still hit the open road together, but they are getting older now. Our adventures have become fewer and farther between.

My life has changed as well. In many ways my life has become something of a contradiction. Above all, I am a runner. I run—a solitary pursuit—and it is the activity I most treasure. However, I have also become somewhat of a public figure, at least in certain circles, which doesn't exactly go hand in hand with a solitary pursuit.

Like many people, I've always wanted to write a book. It was just something I had on my proverbial "life list," along with skydiving, visiting the pyramids, learning a foreign language, hiking the Pacific Crest Trail, and a cadre of other ambitions. So I wrote the book, checked it off the bucket list, and left it at that. If I sold ten copies to my buddies, I'd be lucky. After all, who wants to read about some obscure guy off running hundreds of miles across the most godforsaken terrain on earth? No one, right?

Wrong. *Ultramarathon Man* landed on the *New York Times* bestseller list. Next thing I knew, my "story" was out in the open, my insulated private life all but blown to smithereens. I guess in writing about doing the things I love, about following my heart and setting my own course in life, I somehow gave others permission to do the same. Runners and nonrunners alike flocked to my story, and my once very solitary life suddenly became a little less so.

That is why I look forward to all-night running escapades now more than ever. There is no greater therapy for me than to escape the trappings of humanity and embark on an adventure where I follow my own course freely. These long runs recharge my batteries and leave me feeling rejuvenated and ready to step back into the unexpected life that I now find myself living.

Please don't get me wrong, my so-called "fans" are mostly great people, many of who are accomplished athletes themselves. It's just that while I can run for hours on end without a problem, signing books for hours on end requires a different sort of endurance. As someone who is fairly introverted by nature, it takes a lot out of me spending time immersed in large masses of humanity for extended periods. I don't like being the center of attention. In fact, at times, I don't like attention at all.

As liberating as being the master of my own destiny is, I sometimes think these long solitary runs are a form of running away from myself, basically escaping this new life I've created for a brief reprieve. Out here on the open road nobody knows who I am; and that's just the way I like it.

And tonight's run felt especially rejuvenating. The moon was full and big in the sky.

My wife, Julie, has always insisted that strange occurrences happen during full moons. As I departed the city that evening, a colossal white orb gradually rose to prominence, silhouetting the San Francisco skyline and highlighting the buildings' contours with striking clarity. The moon tonight seemed exquisitely large, and the naked eye could easily discern the craters and pockmarks marring its surface.

The autumn air was unusually dry and warm; I thought about how peculiar it was to be so comfortable while crossing the notoriously blustery Golden Gate Bridge. Tonight was strange, make no mistake.

My path was a familiar one. After reaching the North Headland, I diverted onto a narrow footpath that crosses under the bridge and proceeds up into the trails of Marin County. The rumble of traffic slowly faded away as I ran, eventually replaced by the rustling of tree branches and the sounds of small animals dashing for cover as I glided by.

Once in the wild, I switched on my headlamp to help illuminate the dirt terrain, though I scarcely needed it given the moonlight. The hills around me were bathed in a molten silver hue; they rolled on forever like giant waves in a massive sea.

I ran through the headlands for miles, completely engrossed in the natural beauty of the surroundings. I'd been going for hours when I reached the paved road, though I hardly felt tired at all.

The junction where the trail meets the road was quiet. Besides offering a more pastoral route, using the trail network I'd just been on had allowed me to bypass some of the busy roads of the Bay Area and emerge here at this lesser traveled back road in Marin County. The footpath deposited me onto a quiet two-lane road, which I would follow farther west into even more remote stretches of highway later on in the night. The further removed from automobile traffic I could get, the better.

It would have been possible to remain on the trail even farther into the countryside, but I needed to resupply. My route was calculated. Near the exit point of the trailhead lay the last vestige of humanity, the final signs of intelligent life before disappearing into complete darkness: a liquor store.

Okay, it isn't the ideal place for an endurance athlete to restock, but, hey, it was the only option available.

If you've ever frequented such esteemed establishments late at night, you know the majority of after-hours business comes from the sale of cigarettes and booze. I was after neither.

Upon entering the store, I didn't see anyone. The checkout counter was cluttered with displays of libations and "fine" spirits, many of which were available in single-size containers for less than a buck. Apparently somebody other than McDonald's offers "value pricing."

From behind the displays, a head peeked out, startling me. I jumped. After my initial recoil, I took a look at him and realized he'd been examining me all along, as if grasping for some frame of reference to place "my type." He craned his head, inspecting me from head to toe. Nothing appeared to register. He offered neither smile nor frown.

I said hello and he uttered an indiscernible response, still wary of my presence. Walking down the aisle, I could feel his eyes following me, tracking my every movement. He was a tall man, dark and tan, with facial hair, though not the typical razor stubble of the unkempt; instead he had longer strands that flowed down freely from his chin. His eyes were piercing, as though he had seen things that made him suspicious of even the most seemingly harmless subjects. I got the sense that his primary concern tonight was avoiding being held up at gunpoint.

At the bottom of the candy rack, the token energy bar choices sat covered in dust. Did I care that they were all stale? Heck no. I grabbed a few of them, along with a couple packages of almonds. In the small medical section of the store, I noticed a bottle of Pedialyte. Designed for children suffering from diarrhea and vomiting, in a pinch it is the ultimate athletic rehydration beverage. Gatorade is glorified sugar-water by comparison.

I brought my items to the checkout counter where I discovered, much to my delight, a bowl of overripe bananas. "How much are the bananas?" I asked.

"What are you doing?" he replied sternly.

"Ah . . . asking about the price of the bananas?" I said.

"What are you doing now? It's dark out." He was taken aback by the fact that I was out running at this time of night, but there was earnest inquisitiveness in his eyes, a genuine curiosity. "Are you one of those marathon people?" he asked.

"Ah . . . yes . . . I guess you could say that."

"I used to run when I was a boy," he said. "I want to start again. How far do you go?"

"Tonight?" I didn't want to tell him I was going forty or fifty miles, fearing this might dampen his enthusiasm. "Well . . . let me explain . . . "

Thankfully he broke in before I got any further. "I'm going to start again." He began tallying my purchases and putting the items in a bag. "I'm going to start tomorrow morning," he concluded.

"About those bananas," I asked. "How much are they?"

He seemed troubled by my question. "Take as many as you want, my friend."

I started putting bananas in my bag one by one, presuming they were free, though not entirely sure. He kept talking about starting to run again, and I patiently listened to him. Finally, I cleared my throat (only so many bananas could fit in the bag). "Good luck with it," I said. "You seem pretty determined."

My words dislodged him from his reverie. He blinked a few times and refocused on me. "I'm going to start running again," he said with conviction.

Personally, I believed the man.

Once outside, I opened the Pedialyte and emptied it into the internal bladder of my backpack. I scarfed down two bananas and one stale energy bar, then stashed the rest of the food in my pack for later on. Cinching the shoulder straps, I resumed forward progress.

As I ran, I thought about the unique power running seemed to have to break down barriers and unite people in strange and wonderful ways, regardless of race, creed, socioeconomic status, or age. I was just one of those "marathon people," and he was just a clerk in a liquor store, but we had shared a moment together, and it was good.

Onward and outward I progressed, deeper into the countryside, the full moon now directly overhead. I passed through the small outpost of Nicasio, population 287, and proceeded farther into the boonies, the closest town now miles away. All was going splendidly until I heard the rumble of an approaching vehicle and realized that it was 2:15 A.M. While these backcountry roads are typically quiet at night, I've learned that you need to pay particular attention around this time. You see, the bars let out at 2:00 and people don't want to use the main thoroughfares because they've been doing something they shouldn't be doing before getting behind the wheel. In an effort to avoid getting caught, they use these backcountry routes as alternatives.

Abruptly, a car came whizzing around the corner, heading right for me, which was nothing too unusual. After all, who's expecting to find someone out here jogging at 2:15 in the morning?

But I was pretty lit up. I was wearing a reflective vest and a bright LED headlamp. A flashing red blinker was attached to the shoulder strap of my pack, and I carried a powerful flashlight in my hand. I was hard to miss; I mean, I looked like a running Christmas tree, for crying out loud!

But the car did not veer from its course. In such circumstances, my MO is to give the car a quick shine in the windshield with my flashlight, alerting the driver that there's someone out here running. I gave the quick shine. The car kept coming for me.

Here's when I made the executive decision that diving off the roadside would be a good idea. I turned to launch, but there was a solid embankment next to me. Nowhere to jump.

Then things started happening really quickly. The car was bearing down on me at warp speed with no sign of changing course. My mind was awhirl with disjointed thoughts as I tried to decide whether to go left, right, or *what*. It's hard to keep your cool when you're head-faking a two-ton piece of steel barreling toward you at fifty miles per hour. At some point, I simply closed my eyes and hoped for the best.

The car whizzed by so closely that I could feel the heat of its radiator on my thigh. I stood there counting my blessings, mostly just happy to still be alive.

Then I got a little peeved. The driver must have seen me; he'd been toying with me. This realization made me angry, so I turned toward the speeding vehicle and thrust my fist into the air at it (it was a decent fist, no digits extended).

The driver slammed on the brakes.

Uh-oh, I said to myself, *maybe I shouldn't have done that.*

The car shifted into reverse, and my heart skipped a beat. This was it. There was no place to run, nowhere to hide. I was certain I'd meet my destiny right here on this lonely roadside in the middle of nowhere.

The car came screeching to a halt right next to me. This maniac woman jumped out of the driver's side and ran around the front of the car. She whipped open the passenger door and started riffling through a bag that was sitting on the seat.

Standing there, paralyzed by fear, I waited to see whether she'd pull a knife, a gun, or another type of weapon. How would the end come?

She pulled out . . . a copy of my book. I couldn't believe it. She looked at the picture of me on the cover and then glanced up at my face. "You're him!" she proclaimed. "You're that crazy marathon guy. Oh, my boyfriend just loves you. It's such a coincidence. I just bought him a copy of your book. You gotta sign it!"

Handing me the book, she placed a pen in my trembling hand. I stood there in absolute shock, my face white as a ghost, completely unable to compute any of this.

"His name is Bob," she informed me. "Write something inspirational."

The first thought that popped into my mind was to write:

BOB,

YOUR GIRLFRIEND'S A TOTAL PSYCHO. GET OUT WHILE YOU CAN, BRO.

Then I decided that might not be such a wise idea. I simply signed Bob's book with some words of encouragement and handed it back to her. "Oh, thank you, thank you!" she said. "You have no idea how much this will mean to him."

She took the book, chucked it back into the car, slammed the door, bounced gaily around the front of the vehicle, got in, and drove off into the darkness as though nothing happened.

I was left standing in a dust cloud, wondering what on earth had just transpired. I started fumbling through my pack for a bolt of whiskey, but then I remembered that I don't drink. If I did, now would have been an appropriate time to imbibe heavily.

• • • •

These types of random and unexpected encounters had become increasingly commonplace—some people thinking I hung the moon, others thinking I'd come to rob their liquor store. Stepping back from it all, I attempted to rationally understand the colorful direction my life had taken. But it was no use; things had become too bizarre for me to make any rational sense of it.

Better to just stick with what I knew, I concluded. So I did the one thing I know how to do: I checked my headlamp, tightened my shoelaces, and started putting one wobbly foot in front of the other.

When all else fails, start running . . .

► Checking the course during a multiday run

Follow Dreams, Not Rules

"Make voyages. Attempt them. There's nothing else."

—TENNESSEE WILLIAMS

AND RUN I HAVE. On all seven continents, twice over, I have run. In some of the most remote and exotic places on earth I have run: the Atacama Desert, Patagonia, Mount Fuji, the Australian outback, Namibia, the Gobi Desert, Mont Blanc, the Sahara, Antarctica, New Jersey (okay, maybe not the most remote and exotic of locations, but there's certainly no shortage of unusual native wildlife).

With the success of my first book and my growing notoriety, I saw a once-in-a-lifetime opportunity to turn what I loved to do—running and racing across the globe—into what I *do* (i.e., turn my passion into my vocation). Pioneering aviator Charles Lindbergh once said, "It is the greatest shot of adrenaline to be doing what you've wanted to do so badly." Hallelujah, brother! I took a permanent leave of absence from my day job, walked out the door, and started running.

Life can be either a safe and secure spectator sport or a sometimes risky but amazing adventure. After more than a decade of dabbling part-time, I threw caution to the wind and went for the latter, the great leap into the unknown, quitting my cushy corporate job and dedicating myself to somehow making running a full-time gig. Who needed the plush corner office, the perks, the matching 401(k), and the company car, anyway? These things weren't providing me security, they were creating a prison. George Lucas put it succinctly: "We are all living in cages, with the door wide open." One day I noticed the gate was ajar, so out I ran . . .

• • • •

As any runner can tell you, the playing field in our sport can be rather large. Infinite, really. There is no out-of-bounds, no end zones. You veer off the fairway in our sport, and the rough can stretch on for hundreds of miles. Often, that's where things get the most interesting.

As the fictional Forrest Gump recounted, he decided to go for a "little" run for no reason whatsoever. When he reached the end of the street, he decided to just keep going. And when he got to the end of town, he decided he'd keep on going just a little farther—to the county line. And since he'd run that far, he decided he'd just keep running to the state line. He ran all the way across Alabama for no good reason. He ran all the way to the coast. And when he arrived, he thought, as long as he'd already come so far, he might as well just keep on going. So he turned around and headed the other way. Why not?

If Forrest could do it, I could try.

My meanderings tended to be nearer the fringes than the middle of the road. Navigating along the edge is what I loved the most. Of course, having a faithful caddy to guide you successfully along can be an added nicety. Problem is, in the dozen or so years leading up to my full-time vocation as a runner, most of my friends had figured me out, and they wanted nothing to do with my craziness.

As my running progressed over the years, I constantly searched for new recruits. The surprise came when I discovered an appetite for adventure in the most unlikely candidate, a former college mate of my mine, Topher Gaylord. Unlikely, I say, because he was not a runner at all. Never would I have anticipated his acceptance of my invitation to support me on an all-night run. It's not that Topher wasn't adventuresome—for he was—but he just wasn't a "runner."

I first met Topher back in the eighties in the quaint seaside community of Santa Cruz on the Northern California coast. I was standing in my wetsuit preparing to go windsurfing when a late-model car pulled into the nearby parking lot with a windsurf board on top. What puzzled me most was that I couldn't see the driver. Whoever it was, his or her head was below the steering wheel.

When the driver popped out, I couldn't believe my eyes. He looked to be all of twelve or thirteen—he was actually sixteen at the time—and he weighed eighty-five pounds. Literally. I considered walking over to offer my assistance in lifting the heavy board off the roof but decided instead that it would be amusing to just stand by and watch the disaster unfold. Much to my amazement, he hoisted the weighty rig from the rooftop and set it down gingerly on the sand. I stood there in disbelief, entirely perplexed as to how this little kid had so effortlessly manhandled that bulky windsurf board. I knew right then that I was going to like him.

The youngest of ten, Topher was the quintessential "runt of the litter." Growing up in a commune in Berkeley during the late sixties, he had learned to fend for himself. Our friendship blossomed during college, and I found him to be self-reliant and a quick study. However, I did detect a particular vulnerability in his nature, a character flaw that one day I thought I might be able to exploit: Topher was very trusting of me. Perhaps too trusting.

Being the oldest child in my family, I was extremely adept at discovering such susceptibilities. My younger brother, Kraig, though gullible, had figured me out long ago. Kraig had played the sucker way too many times as I dragged him along on farfetched escapades throughout our childhood. Now my welcome with him was worn out. He knew better.

Topher was fresh game. He was unfamiliar with my ploys and naive to my ways, and the underlying dynamics at play in our relationship soon became happily clear to me. He was the surrogate younger brother. Over the years we had known each other, I'd never invited him to accompany me on any of my running adventures, knowing that the first experience would likely be his last. Once fooled, twice a fool, or so the saying goes.

But at least for one adventure, he was mine.

It was the early nineties and a mutual friend of ours was celebrating his wedding reception in a town near San Francisco, where we lived. I wanted to do something memorable to commemorate the occasion and figured that this would be the perfect opportunity to cash in that chip I had with Topher and bring him along for the ride. I convinced him that the highest form of praise we could bestow upon this new union was to venture to the occasion under our own duress. Human power, if you will. He was a surprisingly easy sell, buying into my suggestion without much need for convincing. Of course, I didn't mention to him that the reception was seventy-five miles away.

Let the games begin!

I departed on foot the next afternoon. Our plan was for Topher to leave later in the day after work, on his bike, and catch up to me during the night. He knew the route I was following and was riding his mountain bike with specially equipped "slick" tires (essentially a narrower profile tire with a flatter tread pattern than the traditionally knobby mountain bike tires), which make riding on paved roads more comfortable.

Unfortunately, it turned out that slicks pop more easily than knobby tires.

Topher had already punctured his back tire and had used one of the pair of replacement inner tubes he'd brought along. Now, alone somewhere along the most remote stretch of highway on our route, another tire ruptured. When he stopped to replace it, he was shocked to learn that it wasn't just one tire: Both of his tires had burst simultaneously. He had no back up.

Never one to panic, he decided to call his girlfriend, Kim, for a lift. However, his cellphone had limited reception. He was too deep in the countryside, well outside of cell range. (In the mid-nineties, coverage was sparse, if not entirely nonexistent, in much of the California backcountry.)

Being the enterprising young lad that he was, Topher hopped up onto the guardrail along the road and held the phone high above his head while balancing himself on the narrow railing. When he looked up at his outstretched arm, he could see one bar of reception.

Slowly, he pulled his arm down to make the call. But just as the phone neared his ear, the bar disappeared. He tried again, more slowly this time. Same thing. He tried once more, this time standing on his tiptoes on the guardrail in an attempt to elevate his head closer to the point of reception. To his great delight, the call went through. He could hear static and crackling on the other end. He glanced up at the phone in an effort to optimize his position. As he did so, his foot slipped and he came crashing down with a horrible thud, one leg straddling each side of the railing. The pain was so horrific that he felt he might have permanently lost the ability to produce offspring.

Panting and trying to regroup, he decided to wait for the help of a passing motorist. That made sense. Getting reception out here was impossible.

An hour went by with no cars. Bummer.

Topher was starting to get cold, not to mention mentally unstable. Instinct took over. Primitive, mindless instinct, the kind that gets people into trouble. With fingers so numb he could barely clench a fist, he hastily hauled his bike as far off the road as possible and crawled into the nearby thicket, curling up underneath a canopy of small branches for warmth. A minute later, he was asleep. Growing up in a commune had conditioned Topher to be one of the quickest sleepers I have ever encountered. When a brief window of opportunity presented itself amongst the childhood chaos, he slept. Topher is the only person I'd ever witnessed fall asleep midsentence—while *he* was talking. The last thought he had before nodding off under that bush was of "Kimmy" and where she might be.

Kim was the glue that kept Topher's life together. Efficient and resourceful, she was not only a tremendous planner, but she always came through in a pinch. That would have likely been the case tonight as well, except that her flight from the East Coast—originally scheduled to arrive at noon—was delayed and she hadn't arrived at San Francisco Airport until the evening.

When she called Topher's cellphone and it rolled directly to voicemail, she had a premonition that something was up. Topher was good at following instructions, and the third item on the list she had compiled and left on the kitchen table for him before her departure read:

3) CHARGE CELLPHONE.

So she was relatively confident he hadn't run out of battery power. What could it be? Then she remembered the route he was following. She knew it would take him relatively far out into the countryside and had an inkling that cell reception might be limited. Actually, she knew that was the case *and* that he was in trouble.

An hour later, Kim was driving through the region, extremely concerned. What troubled her most was that Toph's cellphone still rolled directly into voicemail. He should have passed through this remote backcountry section by now and emerged nearer to humanity and better cell coverage. Had he dropped his phone?

No sooner did this thought cross her mind than she caught a glimpse of something shiny in her headlights off the side of the road. Call it intuition, label it serendipity, tag it a sixth sense; I'll just refer to it as the "magic of Kimmy." Miraculously, she had spotted Topher's bicycle sitting in a heap on the roadside. She pulled over, grabbed a headlamp, and started searching frantically. She spotted his feet first, sticking out from under a bush. She giggled, knowing immediately that he was okay, just sleeping.

Bending down, she began squeezing his toes intermittently, the way a coyote might take a few preparatory gnaws before launching into a full-fledged chomp.

Terrified, Topher sprang awake. He shot up and found himself engulfed in a spider's web of twigs and small branches. Oblivious to his whereabouts, he started screaming and batting at the branches uncontrollably.

Kimmy watched him in amusement. Finally, when he had calmed down and composed himself, she said, "What have you gotten yourself into now, Gaylord?"

"Kimmy, I'm sooo glad to see you," he spouted. "Ahh . . . glad to hear your voice. How do I get out of here?"

"I'm not sure, Toph. It looks like you and that bush have a pretty intimate relationship."

As well-organized and businesslike as she could be, Kimmy was never beyond having some fun. Her striking indigo eyes and beaming smile convey her mischievous nature. Kimmy has the uncanny ability to switch from being a tough-ass negotiator to a practical joker in the blink of an eye. She does so with a natural grace and poise that frequently leaves those on the other side of the bargaining table completely befuddled.

"This is no time to mess around," Topher barked. "Now crawl under this bush and let's engage in a little roadside romance."

"I think you and that plant are doing just fine," she retorted. "Besides, where's Karno?" (Many of my friends had taken to calling me Karno, a truncation of my last name.)

"Oh, man . . . Karno!" Topher rubbed his forehead. "We need to go find him."

"Where did you leave him?" Kimmy asked.

"My tires popped before I caught up with him. He's out there all alone."

"Good thing I grabbed those coffee beans off the table," Kimmy proclaimed. "Let's go!"

Topher dragged himself out from under the bush. They stowed his bike in the back of the pickup and took off down the highway, in search of me.

▶ Topher and Dean at dawn
after running all night
1996

3.0

Are You High?

"Exercise is for people who can't handle drugs and alcohol."
—LILY TOMLIN

WHY DOES PAIN HURT? It's an interesting question, and one that's muddled by the fact that the very definition of pain is elusive. Only the person who experiences the pain can even come close to defining it. Pain is in the neurons of the beholder.

The same can be said of the elusive "runner's high." Some people claim to experience this phenomenon quite regularly; others doubt such a thing even exists. Scientific research on the subject has been *painfully* inconclusive. While researchers in Germany used PET scans to demonstrate that something was going on in the brain during exercise, the precise mechanisms could not be mapped or defined. Other scientists theorize that the "high" comes from completing a challenge rather than as a result of exertion.

There is, however, a general consensus that if something is taking place, it's likely related to the release of endorphins. Endorphins are powerful opioid compounds produced by the pituitary gland and hypothalamus during certain occurrences, such as strenuous exercise, pain, consumption of spicy foods, and, get this, orgasm. Resembling opiates in their ability to produce analgesia and feelings of well-being, endorphins work as natural pain relievers.

This leaves us with an interesting dichotomy. Running causes pain, but it also cures it. So why engage in an activity that causes discomfort only to require more of that very action to bring relief? Isn't that the very definition of addiction?

Perhaps so. That argument would appear valid if you're content cruising through life in the comfort zone. But there are some people who are drawn to dramatic mood swings—deep and dark lows followed by explosive episodes of supreme elation. Anyone who has run a marathon can relate to this firsthand.

The *Wall Street Journal*'s David Wessel writes, "If Van Gogh or Mozart had been on Prozac, would they have been spared the agony of depression, or would the world have been denied their great art?" Modern society—in particular the massive pharmaceutical industry—tells us that pain is bad and needs to be eliminated. I'm not so sure.

Runners have some of their most profound revelations in the darkest grips of pain. What if we were to shift our mind-set and invite pain into our lives, welcome it and meet it head to head on our own terms rather than pop a pill to try to avoid it?

After all, pain is inevitable. Suffering, however, is optional.

Instead of seeking comfort, runners approach the very edge of chaos. As the ravages of potentially debilitating pain take hold, the runner fights to overcome and command the very force that threatens to bring him to his knees. "The obsession with running is really an obsession with the potential for more and more life," the great runner-philosopher George Sheehan once wrote.

The emotional swings that running creates can induce great bursts of creativity and insight. I believe these dramatic changes build strength of character. Just as a problem-free life never makes a strong and good person, smooth roads never make a good runner. As the runner fights the urge to stop, she masters her very mind. In overcoming adversity, she better understands the inner workings of her psyche. Life becomes bigger, bolder, filled with greater potential. "In the middle of difficulty lies opportunity for growth," Einstein wrote.

I've said it before: There's magic in misery. We runners lust for more. Our emotional discord heightens as we approach the fringes. Nothing seems to quell the insatiable appetite for more and more life. We are never thoroughly satisfied. Addiction? Perhaps. Is this a bad thing? You be the judge.

The Marathon Monks of Mount Hiei seek enlightenment through meditation and endurance running. These dramatic shifts in state of mind are fundamental to their Buddhist practice. By subjecting themselves to a cycle of extreme suffering and quiet contentment, they are able to break through to a higher level of being. Such profound "awakenings" have extraordinary implications that carry over to their ability to overcome traditional human limitations, such as pain and discomfort. Their "maintenance program" includes standing idle under a waterfall of ice runoff for hours at a time, a practice that would leave most Westerners in a coma—that is, *if* we could even withstand the shocking cold for more than ten seconds without jumping out of the way. To the enlightened monk, the extreme pain and discomfort the cold creates do not register. The monks have moved beyond these restraining emotions. It makes the sting of interval training look like a cakewalk by comparison.

So, for those out there who would say that runners are addicts, constantly jonesing for our next fix, I would counter, "Yeah, so what of it?" We might be compulsive, obsessive addicts, floating around all day in a haze of endorphins, but that's just the way we like it.

4.0

The Reunion

"A true friend is someone who thinks that you are a good egg even
though he knows that you are slightly cracked."

—Bernard Meltzer

WHEN TOPHER AND KIMMY eventually found me, I
wouldn't say I was at my best. Funny what running for twelve hours
straight can do to a guy's sunny disposition. I think they could tell.

"Want some company, Karno?"

"Sure, misery loves company. Especially if that company is
bearing food. Got any?"

"Oh, shoot," Topher chided, "we totally blew it!"

"Gaylord, I've killed men for less. Tell me you didn't forget the
sacred beans!"

Kimmy produced the bag of chocolate-covered coffee beans she
had grabbed off the kitchen table, and all was suddenly forgiven. If
you've never tried eating chocolate-covered espresso beans after

running sixty miles, you really owe it to yourself. It's about as close to a divine experience you can get without needing to attend confession afterward.

I took off running down the road with the bag of goodies in my hand. A short time later, their car pulled up alongside me again, and out popped not Topher but . . . Kim.

She fell into stride next to me, and we ran side by side into the darkness. I didn't anticipate she'd last more than forty-five minutes, an hour tops. But we got swept up in the moment, mesmerized by the spontaneity of the situation and carried away by the enchantment of the midnight setting. We ran through vast grazing lands. We saw herds of sheep sauntering dreamily across open pastures.

As pleasant as the setting was, the car was within easy access and I was certain my running partner would soon seek its refuge. A verse from a Dr. Seuss poem kept popping into my head as we ran:

> *The moon was out and we saw some sheep.*
> *We saw some sheep take a walk in their sleep.*
> *By the light of the moon, by the light of a star;*
> *They walked all night from near to far.*
> *I would never walk. I would take a car.*

Fourteen miles later, as we arrived at the small outpost of Healdsburg, I was blown away. Kimmy was still by my side. Never did she get back in the car.

"Thanks, Karno, that was great," she said.

"Man, I'm amazed. I can't believe you ran that far with me."

"Me neither. I certainly wasn't planning on it."

• • • •

Thankfully, I'd had the foresight to book a couple of hotel rooms in Healdsburg so we could freshen up. A nap would have been nice, too, but we didn't want to miss out on the best food selections. It was nearing noon, and the reception was scheduled to begin in an hour.

My wife, Julie, had driven up that morning to meet us, and off we dashed to the gathering. The reception was held at the groom's family's estate, a sprawling affair complete with a private vineyard. An orchestra was playing when we arrived. Our timing was impeccable; we made it just in time for the opening round of the buffet.

On our third pass through the line, I asked Kimmy how she was holding up.

"I'm definitely sore. But it was worth it. Maybe next time we'll get Topher to run with us," she concluded.

"*Run?*" Topher said. "You kidding? Unless hornets are chasing me, I'll leave the running to the two of you."

As slight as he was, Topher was remarkably strong for his size. We frequented the gym together, and his strength-to-weight ratio was astounding. He could handily bench-press twice his weight. His lower half, however, was a different story. He had bird legs. The toothpicklike appearance of his legs approached comical proportions. We used to joke that my wrists were bigger than his calves. A runner, he wasn't.

"Don't be so quick to dismiss running, Gaylord, you might actually find it fulfilling. Remember what Nietzsche said: 'That which does not kill us makes us stronger.'"

"Yeah," he responded, "if the experience doesn't leave you maimed, I'd tend to agree with the man. But really, I'm not sure how much stronger I'd be when I'm permanently incapacitated. Running won't make me stronger. It will make me an invalid."

He had a point. Still, I thought there was an inner runner in everybody, young or old, strong or weak, mentally stable or otherwise (perhaps even better if they were otherwise).

I shoveled some roasted veggies on my plate. The buffet offerings were incredible, but there seemed to be heavy emphasis on vegetables and noodles. I was a carnivore who'd been running for most of the past day: I wanted meat.

Topher swung around and saw the waitress approaching. On her tray was a solitary hors d'oeuvre: a single, succulent baby back rib. She offered it to him.

"Wait!" I protested. "He's a vegetarian."

She pulled the tray back and started moving it my way.

"No I'm not!" He reached for the rib again.

Now she was confused. She looked his way, then mine, and in that instant of hesitation he reached over and snatched the morsel.

Before he could put it in his mouth, I broke in. "Let me tell you a story," I quickly interrupted. "A fox, a wolf, and a bear went hunting, and each got a deer. A discussion followed about how to divide the spoils. The bear asked the wolf how he thought it should be done. The wolf said everyone should get one deer. The bear ate the wolf. Then the bear asked how the fox proposed to divvy things up. The fox offered the bear his deer and said the bear ought to take the wolf's deer as well.

" 'Where did you get such wisdom?' the bear asked the fox.

" 'From the wolf,' replied the fox."

Topher looked at me oddly. "Oo-kay," he said, drawing out the *o*. "What . . . exactly . . . are you trying to tell me, Karno?"

"I'm merely expounding upon the virtues of vegetarianism."

My response confused him. Perfect: The deception was working.

I went on. "You see, if the wolf didn't eat meat, his life would have been spared. He never would have selfishly asked for one of the deer to consume."

He looked at me, miffed. I was babbling senselessly. The sleep deprivation and extreme exhaustion of running all night had impaired the delicate workings of my brain and I'd become unraveled. And desperate. I wanted that rib!

He moved it closer to his lips.

"Wait!" I pleaded. "Remember the wolf . . . "

It was too late. He put the entire piece in his mouth and stripped away the flesh in a single bite, the way a T. rex might rip the meat off the vertebrae of some lesser creature. Barbeque sauce dripped down his chin. He looked at the waitress and me, both of us staring at him, bewildered by his behavior, and then he let out an audible growl. Flesh dangled from between his teeth.

"Gaylord," I mouthed, almost unable to get the word out, "that was uncalled for. We could have genially divided it in two. After all, we're not cavemen."

He licked his lips. "Do you happen to have a toothpick?" he asked the waitress. "I think I missed a couple pieces."

"Hand me one as well," I requested, "so I can poke his eyes out!"

"What's going on over here?" Kimmy and Julie had witnessed the incident from across the way and approached us.

"He took my food," I cried.

"Possession's nine-tenths of the law, bro," Topher said.

"Are we going to have to separate the two of you?" Julie asked.

I stared at her, furious. Whose side was she on?

"Are you . . . *all right*?" she asked me. What irked me most was the condescending tone she used, like a mother addressing a child who'd thrown a temper tantrum—which, admittedly, is precisely how I was behaving.

"No," I barked, "I'm not all right." Did these people realize they were patronizing a guy who'd been up all night running? "Look," I went on, "I'm rambling aimlessly, I'm obviously quite delirious, and I could really use some sleep. Plus, I've got this painful chafing in a certain area I can't disclose. So, no, in answer to your question, I'm not . . . *all right*."

Topher thought my response was the funniest thing he'd ever heard. He broke into uncontrollable, hysterical laughter. For a split second I was totally embarrassed. I glanced around nervously to make sure no one was watching. When I looked back at him, I completely lost it as well.

Extreme exhaustion can elicit totally inappropriate behavior. We'd been set off. Nothing could mitigate our laughter; we fed off each other's energy. Tears ran down our cheeks as we stood there in the middle of a swank wedding celebration, cackling uproariously like two clowns. So intense was my laughter that I thought I might suffocate.

"*Ahem.*" Someone behind me cleared his throat. I turned to find the father of the groom. He was a stately gentleman and a very successful businessman. He was wearing a beautifully tailored tuxedo. My first thought was, "That must have been expensive to rent." Then I realized that he probably owned it.

Next to him stood a very dignified-looking woman.

"Dean," he said, "I'd like to introduce you to Dianne Feinstein."

The realization that there was a US senator standing in front of me made me choke, and something, perhaps a small piece of partially chewed carrot, shot embarrassingly from my nose. She reeled at the sight, and a very awkward moment of silence ensued, the nasal-ejection incident freezing time.

I stood there in utter horror, paralyzed with embarrassment and not sure what to do. In my current state of exhaustion, I was unfit to be in any public place, let alone standing face-to-face with an elected official.

"Nice meeting you," Senator Feinstein eventually said politely, then raised her eyebrows, indicating to the groom's father her overwhelming desire to move on quickly.

They walked off.

The episode was sobering. A feeling of nausea swept over me. I turned to my party and said, "I'm not feeling so well. Let's get some fresh air."

"Hon," my wife reminded me, "we're standing outside."

The four of us walked toward the outskirts of the gathering and found a private area. Topher turned to me and took inventory. Clearly I was in a state of shock. "Dude, why the long face?" he asked.

"You saw what happened in there."

"Look at it this way, Karno: How many people ever get the opportunity to make a complete fool of themselves in front of an elected official? You jumped at the opportunity. Carpe diem, bro! They say you only get one chance at a first impression. Well, I'm sure she won't be forgetting you anytime soon."

At that moment, I felt an overwhelming urge to hurt the man. But I was quite certain I lacked the energy to chase him down and act upon my impulse.

Instead I said, "Thank you, Topher. I truly appreciate your warm sentiments." I stepped forward, hoping he would drop his guard long enough for me to move within striking range.

But his years of growing up with nine older siblings had taught him well, and the little shit instinctively maintained a safe distance between us.

With any future hopes of a political appointment dashed, we decided the best course of action would be to return to the buffet line for another round. The incident may have battered my pride, but my hunger had emerged unscathed. I wiped my nose with the back of my sleeve; rather than leaving the party hungry and humiliated, I would see to it that I left only humiliated. In desperate times, you embrace any little victory you can get.

5.0

It Only Hurts
When I Run

"This sport would be fun, if it wasn't for all the running."
—**Marathoner's T-Shirt**

ON MY WAY to dropping off my son at school one morning, we passed a jogger. He looked miserable. I asked my son, "Doesn't that just inspire you to want to lace up your shoes and take off for a run?"

"Not really," came his drowsy response.

Truth be told, running isn't always the most pleasant activity. Okay, perhaps it's even a bit agonizing at times. All right, it's sometimes downright *excruciating*.

Of course, we runners aren't necessarily the best advertisements for our sport. I mean, when was the last time you saw someone running down the street laughing aloud (unless you were nearby an insane asylum and one of the inmates happened to have escaped)?

The reality is, even most other athletes loathe running. As one runner once aptly noted, "My sport is your sport's punishment."

Yet, based on my encounters, I've found runners to be a rather lighthearted bunch. Perhaps the agony we experience performing our craft leads to a corresponding humor as counterbalance. You know, a sort of yin and yang thing.

A sign I saw along the course during a recent Chicago Marathon exemplifies this jocular nature. There was a young lady standing on the side of the road holding a large posterboard above her head. It read:

I Am Dan's Athletic Supporter

The sign looked playful, so I'm presuming the double meaning was intentional, but I just chuckled and ran past, not thinking to stop and ask.

Over the years, I've seen a number of classic roadside posters displayed by spectators. Here are a few more notables:

Suck It Up! Running Won't Kill You. You'll Pass Out First.

If It Were Easy, I Would Do It.

And:

Mortuary Ahead. Look Alive.

These aren't the only humorous pronouncements I've absorbed as a runner. Check these zingers:

"The only reason I would take up jogging is so that I could hear heavy breathing again."

—ERMA BOMBECK

"Slow and steady wins the race . . . except in a real race!"

—HIGH SCHOOL TRACK COACH

"Why couldn't Pheidippides have died at mile twenty?"

—FRANK SHORTER

"When the going gets tough, the sprinters quit!"

—MID-SEVENTIES LONG-DISTANCE TRACK TEAM POSTER

"Start slow . . . and taper off."

—WALT STACK'S ADVICE ON RUNNING A MARATHON

I once posed the following request on my weekly *Runner's World* blog: "If you know of any upbeat running quotes, please share." I received hundreds of enthusiastic responses. Here are some noteworthy quips:

"Want a strong, solid relationship that is willing to go the distance? Get to know your running shoes."

—LONELY LONG-DISTANCE RUNNER

"Life is short . . . running makes it seem longer."

—BARON HANSEN

"Getting motivated can be tough, especially when you're not motivated."

—YOURS TRULY

I saw this one on the T-shirt of a guy picking up his race number at the New York City Marathon expo:

"Tell me why I decided to do this again?"

Then there's the infamous Maurice Greene quote:

"Every morning in Africa a gazelle wakes up. It knows it must move faster than the lion or it will not survive. Every morning a lion wakes up and it knows it must move faster than the slowest gazelle or it will starve. It doesn't matter if you are the lion or the gazelle, when the sun comes up in Africa you better be moving."

A Nor Cal girls' cross-country team T-shirt pretty much says it all:

"Yeah, I run like a girl. Try and keep up."

Being an ultramarathoner, I'm especially drawn to funny references about our particular brand of locomotion:

"Any idiot can run a marathon; it takes a special idiot to run an ultra."

—IDIOTIC, BUT HAPPY, ULTRA RUNNER

"If you start to feel good during an ultramarathon, don't worry, you'll get over it."

—GENE THIBEAULT

"Why run one hundred miles? Because basketball and baseball only require one ball."

—**Kim Gaylord**

Letterman has his Top Ten. Well, touché!

Top Ten Ways You Know You're an Ultra Runner

10) Your feet look better without toenails.

9) Your idea of a fun date is a thirty-mile training run.

8) You're tempted to look for a bush when there's a line for the public restroom.

7) You don't think twice about eating food you've picked up off the floor.

6) Peeing in a toilet starts to seem unnatural.

5) You can expound on the virtues of eating salt.

4) You run marathons for speedwork.

3) You have more buckles than belts. (The prize for finishing most ultras is a belt buckle.)

2) NEXT GAS 36 MILES signs start sounding like tempting runs.

1) You visit a national park with your family and notice a thirty-mile trail connecting where you are with the place your family wants to visit next, which is a hundred-mile drive away, and you think, "Hmm . . . might be faster to lace up."

Perhaps all this humor helps offset the punishment of miles pounding the pavement and hours of disciplined, relentless training.

There is a crazy, conflicted allure to long-distance running. It is at once magical and manic. Running has a way of possessing your soul, infiltrating your psyche, and quietly becoming your central life force. The difference between a jogger and a runner is that a jogger still has control of his life. We runners have lost it.

Is this a bad thing? Like laughter, running has an uncanny ability to mellow the soul, to take the edge off hard feelings and put things back into healthy perspective. Alan Alda once noted: "When people are laughing, they're generally not killing each other." I think the same could be said of running.

Maybe that's just the viewpoint of a naive runner. I'm not really sure. Instead of pondering this question too diligently, I prefer to simply lace up a pair of running shoes and hit the open road. As a runner, that's what I know how to do. To strike out on a trail and just go and go and go like there's no tomorrow; to run until my problems fade beneath my feet and the world becomes new again.

We runners don't need a lot. It is not what we have but what we enjoy that constitutes our abundance. I have found my church, and it is at the end of a long trail on a distant mountaintop. Like many runners, I've discovered it is here that I feel most at peace, entirely content and whole.

"That's all I have to say about that."

—**Forrest Gump**

6.0

Running in the Dark—Naked

"Adversity introduces a man to himself."

—ANONYMOUS

ONE HUNDRED AND eighteen degrees Fahrenheit. That's what the digital temperature gauge on the car's dashboard displayed in red. The clock next to it showed the time to be 10:00 P.M. I'd been on the road the entire day, and the desolate stretch of highway I'd been traveling the past ten miles was so straight I'd used my knee to steer.

No other vehicles had passed me in hours. There'd been no signs of human life; just miles and miles of barren landscape and blowing tumbleweeds along the narrow moonlit highway. Death Valley in the middle of summer doesn't attract many visitors.

In the distance, the dim, yellow lights of a small desert outpost appeared. Whatever it was, this location would be my last opportunity to procure supplies. That is, if it wasn't entirely abandoned like the other buildings I'd passed.

Distances become obscured in the desert at night. What at first appears to be only inches away can actually be several miles away. It took me nearly twenty minutes to reach that roadside station. And I was going ninety-five miles an hour.

When I arrived at the small gas station and opened the car door, a hot blast of wind and sand blew into my face, coating my skin, hair, and teeth with a chalky grit. Death Valley has a personality all its own, and it seemed to be saying to me, "Welcome to paradise, now get out of here."

Although the establishment was barely lit, the door was open, so I walked in. The air inside was dank, though marginally cooler; a tired air conditioner sputtered in the corner.

An older woman sat behind the counter. I said hello, and she just nodded, as if returning the pleasantry would require too much energy.

I looked around the dingy surroundings, hoping to find one particular item. Aha, there it was! In the corner, below the laboring air conditioner, was an icebox. Its thick metal casing was partially corroded and certain areas had begun to rust, but it appeared to be working.

Turning to the woman, I asked, "Do you carry block ice?"

After a brief pause, she said, "Yup."

"Oh, great! How does it come?"

Another brief pause. "In blocks."

"No, no . . . " I tried to clarify. "I mean, does it come in various sizes?"

Another pause. "Nope," she offered, with a hint of irritation.

I tried again. "Well, what size are these blocks?"

"Big," is all she said.

I bought a few bags of big block ice and walked out.

That was my welcome to the enchanting little village of Stovepipe Wells.

After the ice purchase, I set out once again for the small enclave of Furnace Creek, located even deeper in the bowels of Death Valley. It was here that I met my father, who had driven up from Southern California to spend a couple relaxing days with me in "paradise."

"Hello, Popou," I said hugging him. "Popou" means "Grandfather" in Greek. My two kids affectionately refer to my parents as Popou and Yiayia (which is Greek for "Grandmother"), and I have adopted the practice as well.

"Hello, Son."

We checked into our room and tried to get settled in the midnight heat of the desert. Even dialed to its highest setting, the air conditioner in our room seemed overpowered by the residual heat of the day.

As we lay in our beds sweating, he announced to me, "I'm going to play tomorrow morning."

"You're gonna what?"

"I brought my sticks, I'm going to play a round."

"Golf? You've got to be kidding! That's ludicrous. Do you know how hot it will be out there? Is the course even open this time of year?"

"I called earlier in the week and reserved a 6:00 A.M. tee time."

Popou is a fanatical, lifelong golfer. He lives for golf, would play seven days a week if he could. Now that he's semiretired, he sometimes can (and often does).

The allure of playing Furnace Creek, which bills itself as "the World's Lowest Golf Course"—214 feet below sea level, to be precise—was too great an opportunity for him to pass up, mid-summer inferno or not.

"I'll set the alarm on my cellphone and be finished early. Don't worry."

Don't worry, he says to me. People die out here in the middle of summer and he was about to play a round of golf. Needless to say, I was a little more than concerned. So you can imagine my delight when I woke up the next morning to find Popou still snoring away in the bed beside me. The clock read 9:00 A.M. The halcyon haze of the desert warmth, along with the white noise of the droning air conditioner, had lulled the two of us into a dream-state fog, and we'd overslept. Thank goodness.

Popou awoke a few minutes later, confused. "What happened?" he sputtered. He reached for his cellphone. The battery had run out sometime during the night. I was relieved, but tried not to show it. "I'm sorry, Popou, next time." But that didn't stop him. He grabbed the hotel phone and dialed the pro shop. A man answered on the other end. "They're open," Popou said to me. "I'm going."

"But the sun is already up," I protested. "Do you have any idea how hot it will be out there now?"

If there's one thing I've learned over the years, it's that short of military intervention, there are few things that can stop a determined golfer. He bolted out the door.

"Wait," I hollered, "I'm coming with you."

The course was less than a quarter mile away. Popou drove like a maniac to get there. We didn't see a single soul along the way, but he still drove like a madman.

To call what we came upon a "pro shop" would be a gross overstatement. It was more a glorified storage shed. A man sat on a barstool inside with his feet on the counter. He nodded slightly when we walked in, but didn't change his position and kept watching the small, staticky, black-and-white TV propped up in the corner.

Popou rushed over to him. "I overslept and missed my tee time. Can you still get me on?"

The man looked at him curiously. "Let's see," he said, "we haven't had anyone play this course in the past month, so I think there's a pretty good chance we can slot you in."

"Ohh . . . " Popou let out a sigh of relief. "That's great news."

"There's only one problem," Popou confessed remorsefully, "I forgot to bring a collared shirt. Would it be okay to play in a T-shirt just this once?"

The man sat up and looked at Popou. "Buddy, you could play completely naked and no one's gonna care. There's not exactly a gallery of gawking spectators lining the fairways."

"Terrific!" Popou said. "Thank you." I hoped he was thanking him for permission to play the course without a collared shirt, not naked.

"How much are greens fees?" Popou asked.

The man quoted the fees for nine holes.

"How much for eighteen?"

The man looked at Popou dumbfounded. "Geez . . . I dunno. We've never had anyone ask before."

I pulled Popou aside. "Maybe that's a good indication you shouldn't play eighteen holes. No?"

"Are you kidding? Real golfers don't play nine holes!"

"Popou! That's the type of maverick attitude that gets people killed out here. It's going to be 120 degrees!"

"I'll wear a hat."

"Popou! You are a stubborn, bullheaded Greek man."

"Ahem," he cleared his throat. "When was the last time I saw *you* run a half-marathon?"

He had a point. I don't think I'd ever registered for a half-marathon in my life, always opting for the full marathon distance instead. Like father, like son, I guess.

He had played the hypocrisy card, and it won him the hand. Eighteen holes it would be. Thankfully, I had also brought a hat.

• • • •

After spending a few hours on those fairways caddying for him, I was certain that Popou had just completed "the World's Toughest Round of Golf," which was fitting, because I was about to enter "the World's Toughest Footrace," the Badwater Ultramarathon.

That's one name for the race; others just call it hell. Perhaps that's a bit extreme, though if anything warrants such an ominous distinction, running 135 miles in the midsummer inferno of Death Valley would qualify. Passing by places like Hells Gate, Devils Cornfield, Dantes View, Funeral Mountains, Coffin Peak, Starvation Canyon, and Deadman Pass, the point seems to be sufficiently made.

In 1996, there were forty days on which the mercury topped 120 degrees Fahrenheit. That's hot. I should know, because I was out there running during one of them. I'd nearly died during the 1995 event, collapsing on the asphalt at mile seventy-eight and being scraped off the ground and rushed to safety by my crew. I'd pledged to return the next year to avenge my failure (this speaks volumes about my intelligence . . . or lack thereof).

Things were different back in those days. In 1996, the safety precautions were looser than they are today. Nowadays, many of the runners have multiple crew members and several support vehicles to provide assistance along the course. A minimum of two crew members is now required. Back then, it was just Popou and me.

Let me tell you a little bit about Popou. He isn't always the most agreeable of characters, and we've certainly had our share of disagreements over the years. In fact, I sometimes think he enjoys bantering as a form of entertainment. But out here in Death Valley, our periodic squabbles seemed entirely trivial and the true beauty of the man radiated as brightly as the desert sun. You see, the magic of Popou is that he is always there. Even when we're like two old Greeks in a Santorini taverna arguing about the best brand of ouzo, at least we're together. He is the most faithful companion a son could ever ask for.

Growing up, many of my friends' fathers never attended any of our sporting events. Popou, on the other hand, never missed any of mine. I didn't always want him there, but that was only because I had the security of knowing that he always *would* be there.

No matter how disagreeable he can be, there's never a doubt that he'll always be there for me when I need him. For this, I respect and love him deeply. Come hell or high water (in this case, come hell or Badwater), he is always there.

I remember the two of us sitting at the start of that 1996 race, listening to a highway patrolman outlining some practical safety tips for the racers and their crews to follow. He encouraged one of the support crew members to carry an extra car key in his pocket. One of the most common occurrences the officer had encountered during previous Badwater events was people unwittingly locking themselves out of their cars, often while the engine was still running. He explained that in the crews' haste to get aid to their athletes as quickly as possible—compounded by brain-frying heat and sleep deprivation—they jump out of the vehicle, slam the doors to keep the cool air-conditioning inside, and rush over to the assistance of the athlete, forgetting that the car doors can automatically lock. If this happens while the ignition is still on, as it often does, the car eventually runs out of gas, leaving the crew helpless and stranded on the roadside and the athlete without aid.

If he found a party locked out of its car, the officer explained a unique "high-tech" tool he used to enter the vehicle. He held up a roadside rock.

I whispered to Popou, "Be sure to put a spare key in your pocket."

"We don't have one."

That was just one of our many oversights. Another was having only a single Styrofoam cooler. At mile forty-five we stopped along the highway for a brief reprieve. I'd been running for some ten hours straight, and the temperature had reached 122 degrees. Popou pulled out the cooler and set it on the pavement in front of me to prop my legs on. "Good call," I commended him.

I sat on the car bumper with my legs resting atop the cooler. The heat was so intense, however, that it actually felt worse sitting than it did moving forward. So the break only lasted a few short minutes before I resumed my progress.

When Popou lifted the cooler back into the car, the entire contents came spilling out the bottom. The 200-plus-degree asphalt had completely melted the Styrofoam base into a white goo—something akin to the innards of a roasted marshmallow that had fallen off its skewer. It smelled like a smoldering marshmallow, too.

"Bad call," I condemned him, looking at the white mess on the pavement. Now we had no ice.

From there, things went to hell in a handbasket. The car stalled. The wind howled. The sand blew. My sneakers disintegrated. And Popou began to disintegrate as well.

Bless the man, he was out here single-handedly doing the job of several. But it was showing. And rightly so. Ironically, it is often a crew member who overlooks his own needs and ends up in trouble. In fact, crew members end up in the hospital more often than the race participants themselves.

We continued forging numbly through the night, growing increasingly haggard. With each new mile and each passing hour, we began to slur our words and talk nonsensically.

I asked Popou for one of my specialties, thinking that food might perk me up. My "specialty" consisted of an almond butter sandwich on whole-grain nut bread with sliced bananas and honey drizzled in the middle, topped off with a liberal dousing of soy sauce. Sounds gross, right? Wrong. After running a hundred miles nonstop across the desert, it's the finest delicacy on earth.

The food helped for awhile. At least I wasn't throwing up everything I put in my mouth (including water) like I had been the year prior. Hey, when you're clinging to every tattered thread of hope, the little things go a long way. Contents remain in stomach = good. Contents forcefully ejected from stomach = bad.

Dawn brought renewed optimism. That is, until the first rays of sunlight scorched my already burnt skin like a branding iron. Running through the incinerator of Death Valley the day before had been treacherous in surreal ways. The superheated air felt as if a blow-dryer were being held inches from my face. This unrelenting harshness lasted throughout the day and well into the night, drying out my sinuses and leaving my eyeballs parched and irritated. The epithelia lining my mouth had begun to slough off in papery strips, like an iguana shedding its skin, and the pieces were stuck between my teeth. The situation was further compounded by the fact that we'd been without ice. Although we were getting closer to the finish with each step, morale was at an all-time low.

Popou looked like a castaway on a desert island. His skin was ashen and tightly drawn around his cheekbones. His eyes were sullen and sunken deeply in their sockets.

Seeing him like this scared me, and my concern for him was the driving force keeping me alert. I knew he felt this same worry about me. We were entirely reliant upon each other. What had largely begun as my personal battle had morphed into *our* war. We were in this together. We would either succeed or fail as a team.

The first, and really only, township along the course is located at the 122-mile mark. Lone Pine, population 1,488, sits at the base of the arduous climb to the finish, which resides up the side of Mount Whitney. At the base is a local hotel called the Dow Villa. My secret plan was to get a room at the Dow to allow Popou to rest for awhile. My concern for his well-being had reached panic levels.

As we were passing the hotel, I informed him of my intentions.

"What, for me? Are you kidding? I'm not tired."

"Popou, you look like a skeleton."

"Don't stop on my accord. *You* can stop, but I'm not stopping."

"And what, you're going to keep going without me?"

What he was saying made absolutely no sense, which only heightened my concern. But I could see this was going nowhere. Even on his deathbed, Popou would be obstinate.

"Okay, Popou, *I* need to stop. Can you just help me get my stuff to the room before you continue?"

He agreed. When we got to the room I closed the curtains, and it was very dark and cool inside. "Popou, just have a quick seat in that chair over there."

Amazingly, he didn't argue. I watched him sink into the soft folds of the cushioning. It worked better than anesthesia. If he'd been counting down from one hundred he would have made it to about ninety-three before slipping off to sleep.

Almost instantly, he began snoring. I walked over and lay on the bed, lulled by his rhythmic sonatas. But I couldn't sleep. One hundred and twenty-two miles of running had left my metabolism supercharged. Rest was impossible, so I eventually gave up and walked down to the lobby where I located a collection of good books. The hotel was empty, so I sat there and read.

Nine hours later, Popou emerged. He appeared groggy and dazed.

"You okay, Popou?"

"My shoulders are killing me. I need a vanduzzi."

"Here? At the hotel?"

"Do you think you could give me one?"

I thought about it for a moment and concluded that all of the necessary ingredients were within reach. "This is crazy," I said. But

I knew a vanduzzi would restore his health, so I agreed to administer one.

After rounding up all the needed materials, I returned to our room. "Whoops, forgot something. Hold tight," I told him. I ran back down to the front desk and grabbed some matches.

Vanduzzis can be traumatic, especially for first-timers. But Popou was a grizzled vet. He hardly flinched.

After administering the ancient Greek remedy, we headed out the door to tackle the final leg of the journey. He was a new man.

Across the street from the Dow Villa is the world-renowned Lone Pine Pizza Factory. (Okay, maybe not world-renowned, but certainly a big hit in the area.) The Pizza Factory's motto is: "We toss 'em, they're awesome." And I couldn't agree more!

A large Hawaiian–style pizza was the perfect send-off for the final leg of our journey. A pitcher of cold beer would have been a nice complement, but that would have to wait.

We were careful to order the pizza with thin crust, and we instructed them not to slice it. Then I removed the entire thing from the box and rolled it into a continuous Italian burrito, which I mowed as I ran. It was gruesome and messy, sauce dripping everywhere, but it was oh so good!

The finish line was a half-marathon away. Basic, you might say, right? After running 122 miles, what's another thirteen? Problem is, in those remaining thirteen miles you climb the equivalent of a vertical mile straight up into the sky. The official finish line is at 8,360 feet above sea level.

And it was kicking my ass. The first seven miles were survivable, but the steepness of the road and the increasing altitude of the remainder was rapidly taking its toll. I fought to maintain some semblance of forward momentum, grunting and moaning in agony, but my pace was still sluggish at best. Popou looked at me with concern. For once, he seemed at a loss for words. He knew how important it was for me to finish what had nearly finished me a year earlier. He knew this because it was equally important to him.

Onward I labored, growing increasingly weary with each stride. My ears began ringing and my head throbbed. The altitude was crushing my skull. I began staggering and weaving, my entire universe confined to the three feet of road in front of me. I shook my head and screamed at the sky in a desperate attempt to regain coherence.

It didn't work. I spun, took an awkward half step sideways, trying to balance the load, but it was no use. The lateral strain was too much for my weakened leg to support and it buckled under the pressure. I came crashing to the asphalt.

Lying on my back looking up at all the stars twirling around in the heavens, it occurred to me that stars don't twirl. You know better than that, I thought. Then I realized that it was still daylight, and it was just me who was seeing stars. Funny the random thoughts that cross your mind when you're on the verge of entering a coma.

When my eyes cleared, I saw Popou staring down at me. Neither of us moved for a good half minute. I blinked a few times in hopes of clearing the haze. This is good, I thought. As good as it gets, in fact. I looked up at Popou and mouthed, "I love this shit."

Popou just grinned. Didn't say a word. Didn't have to. The look on his face said clearly that he echoed my sentiments. This empowered me with the energy to get to my feet and resume forward progress. Man, I thought, this is living, this is life!

It was approaching nightfall when we rounded the final corner of the course and approached the end. One of the race officials, Matt Frederick, was sitting in a foldable beach chair next to the official finish line, snoozing.

A few campers and hikers were milling about. When they saw us coming, they began clapping and cheering. The commotion woke Matt, who popped to his feet to welcome us.

"Wait, wait," he said as I came within feet of the end. "Let me put up the finish tape."

Popou offered to help him, but one of the hikers grabbed an end of the tape instead and helped Matt stretch it across the finish line.

"Come here, Pops," I instructed. I grabbed his hand and we both went through the tape together.

Matt and the other onlookers congratulated us on the accomplishment. They asked how the race had been, and Popou began sharing stories. I just stood there resting with my hands on my knees, basking in the grand splendor of it all.

"What a man can be, he must be," Abraham Maslow once said. Hunched over, on the verge of collapsing, I was completely fulfilled in knowing that I had been the best me that I could be. Leg muscles quivering, feet battered and bloodied, ears ringing, I couldn't have been happier.

• • • •

Since that pinnacle experience at the finish of the 1996 Badwater Ultramarathon, I've returned to the race seven times over the course of which I've nearly been: run off the road by a maniac driver, struck by lightning, bitten by a rattlesnake in the road at night, taken out by a flash flood, trapped in a freak snowstorm on Mount Whitney, sickened by accidentally drinking nonpotable water, and nearly ended up in the hospital (probably more times than I care to know).

My goal has been to amass ten Badwater Ultramarathon finishes and ten Western States 100-Mile Endurance Run finishes, two of the most grueling endurance races in the world. Since they typically fall just two weeks apart, the recovery period between them is considered rather inadequate (okay, some might say ridiculously so). Having eleven WS 100 finishes under my belt, I needed to complete Badwater three more times to reach my goal.

During an interview, I mentioned this aspiration to a reporter, and a reader subsequently responded by saying that my quest to finish each of these events ten times was overzealous. "Why attempt to be the first to achieve ten finishes of each?" he wrote. "Nobody else has even finished five."

While his point is well taken, he seems to misconstrue my intentions. I'm not doing this to be the *first*, I'm doing it as a personal goal. Being able to finish each of these incredible races ten times is just something I want to accomplish, a life goal, not something I want to prove to anybody else. Over the years I've come to the realization that fulfillment of one's own personal goals is far more gratifying than winning a prize or being first. The latter accomplishment appeases the ego; the former provides inner satisfaction. There really is no comparison. This challenge was about opening the door to my cage and letting myself out.

Finishing is one thing, but placing well is also important to me, and my performances at Badwater have fluctuated over the years. With the responsibilities of managing a growing business, providing for a family, writing a couple of books, trying to remain active in the community, and giving of my time and energy to support local charities, I haven't always found the necessary time to train as diligently as I would have liked.

The year 2009 was going to be different. In the weeks leading up to the '09 Badwater, I was in the best shape of my life. This was the year I made the necessary sacrifices to sufficiently train and prepare for the event.

Popou was pleased. He can be fiercely competitive, and he liked the fact that I was taking this year's race more seriously. He also saw, perhaps for the first time, the cost of what it took to do so. As deeply as I loved the man, I sometimes felt that he discounted the hard work, dedication, and sacrifice required for high achievement. Earn a graduate degree, run a successful business, write a *New York Times* bestseller, win a couple ultra endurance races, yada yada yada . . . that's just dandy. But whaddaya got for me today?

When I first came to recognize this dynamic, I was slightly resentful. What had he made of *his* life that made mine so insufficient?

This resentment, I eventually discovered, was misdirected. He might have come across as saying that nothing I did was ever adequate, but what he was *really* saying is that he sees great promise in me and that, perhaps unlike himself, he wants me to live up to my full potential. Isn't that what every loving father wants for his son? After I recognized this, my resentment subsided and our friendship blossomed.

• • • •

A week before the 2009 Badwater event, Popou went to the doctor, concerned about some recent dizziness and shortness of breath. It turned out he needed immediate open-heart surgery. Suddenly, all that was stable in my life was thrown into an uncontrollable tailspin.

"What?" I demanded over the phone. He had just finished telling me the news. "That can't be, you're in perfect shape."

"Son," he explained, "my coronary arteries are almost entirely occluded. I saw the X-rays. It's not good. The cardiologist said I'm a walking time bomb."

It took me a moment to process this news. "Okay," I finally said, "I'll be right down."

I called Julie and told her what had happened, then booked a flight from San Francisco to Southern California.

Popou was his typically jovial self, but I could sense his concern. Confronting one's own mortality tends to undermine even the most eternally optimistic personalities. He needed something to inspire hope, but all he was getting were endless lab slips and hospital registration forms.

"When are you taking off?" he asked me at the breakfast table the next morning.

"Taking off?"

"For the desert."

"Oh, Popou," I said with a smile, "that's nice of you to ask, but I'm not going to Badwater this year. Not now."

"Don't be crazy," he said. "What are you going to do here, sit around the hospital and watch the nurses bathe me? Seven down, my boy. You've got three to go!"

I thought about what he was saying. "I can't go."

"Son," he said, "I *want* you to go."

"Let's talk about it later. Right now I want to hear about that new Odyssey F7 putter you just got. I heard they're amazing!"

Lying in bed that night, I thought about our conversation. Perhaps he really did want me to go to Badwater. He knew how important it was to me. But maybe it was just as important to him. At seventy-three years old and in failing health, many of his unattained life dreams were probably starting to seem unreachable now. Here I was, vibrant and in top physical condition, ready to tackle "the World's Toughest Footrace" for an eighth time. More importantly, however, I was his son. This was a dream that he could take pride in as well.

Badwater was back on.

• • • •

Sitting in the waiting room, tapping my foot impatiently, I wondered what was taking so long. The nurse had said the doctor would be out shortly. That was an hour ago. My concern was growing with each passing minute. Finally, he arrived.

"How is he?" I asked.

"He's fine. The surgery went well. We had to perform quadruple bypass. Would you like to see him?"

"Oh, would I."

I followed the doctor to the recovery room. "He's still a bit groggy."

I didn't care; I just wanted to see Popou.

What I saw shook me to my foundation. There he was, lying in a hospital bed with endless tubes and needles coming out of his body. His face was withdrawn and pale, his skin sagging from his cheeks as though it was melting.

My first reaction was anger. I wanted to start yelling at the doctor and all of the nurses and assistants scurrying about the room. I wanted to yank out all of those hoses and IV lines coming from my poor father's body.

And then it dawned on me: This wasn't Popou at all. Popou was that gregarious, energetic, sometimes neurotic, but always fiery and fun-loving fellow I knew and loved, not this half-dead skeleton lying before me.

Of course, it *was* Popou. When I finally came to accept this fact, it made me shiver. I tried to talk to him, but it was clear the drugs still hadn't left his system and he didn't reply. So I just stood by his side, feeling helpless and feeble.

"We need to clean him up now," one of the nurses finally said.

I looked at her, slowly realizing that she was telling me to leave. My last thought was to hug Popou. I began reaching for him, but the nurse put out her hand. "Please don't," she said coldly. "You know, risk of infection."

I wept for the entire six-hour drive to Death Valley. I could not control my tears. I could not listen to the radio; I could not return phone calls; all I could do was think of Popou. As independent as my life had become from his—with a wonderfully loving family of my own—I still could not imagine my life without him.

• • • •

Badwater commands one hundred percent focus and concentration. Anything short of that, and you're doomed. My mind and spirit were elsewhere, and I struggled during this race like never before.

My crew was incredible. They could see the mental anguish I was experiencing and they knew the physical toll it was taking on me. My dear friend Michelle Barton had recruited two of her girl-friends to volunteer for the thankless job of getting me across the desert. This was the first time I had met either of her two friends, and they were nothing but supportive. My buddy JT Service had also come out to help. As a sub-2:20 elite marathoner, the ultra scene was like a different dimension to him. He couldn't fathom the idea of running five marathons back-to-back.

Nothing went right in the race. The complex emotional layers seemed as cumbersome as the layers of clothing I was wearing to keep the sun off. By the middle of the night, only halfway through the 135-mile distance, I'd had it.

"I feel so damn confined," I said to JT. "Like I'm stuck in a nightmare and can't escape."

It was approaching 2:00 a.m. and JT was pacing me along a dark and remote stretch of highway. We ran together for a few more minutes of silence. "You know," I went on, "we enter this world naked and with nothing, and we leave this world naked and with nothing. That goes for our emotional baggage along with all the material crap we accumulate."

JT just ran alongside me, not saying a word. He is a good listener, a good friend.

I went on. "I think it would be tremendously liberating to free oneself of all the emotional deadweight we carry around with us. Life is life. We come and we go. No matter how much we stress and strain, there's no altering this course. Still, we remain burdened by so much heavy layering."

"Karno, are you thinking what I'm thinking?"

"Yeah, man. I'm breaking through. I'm dumping all that binds me and runnin' free."

"Shit. That's what I thought. Okay, count me in!"

"Keep your reflective vest on, though," I said, "or else we could be disqualified."

The official rules stated that it was mandatory to wear a reflective vest at night. But they made no mention of other clothing.

"Oh, this feels so good!" I giggled like a child. We had stripped off our clothes and were running naked as the day we were born.

For the first time in days, nothing was chafing me. I had nothing but the shirt on my back (er, the reflective vest on my back), and it felt great. We come into this world bare, and we leave the same way. It would happen to Popou; it would happen to me. Such is the cycle of life.

The best we can do is cherish every moment. If we hold close those we love, their memories will live on within us even after they're gone. It was all about stripping away the complex layers we construct around us and accepting the truth. This revelation set me free.

"Damn, this feels good!" I said to JT.

Just then, the headlights of our crew vehicle came around the corner from behind us. "What the . . . ?" I heard Michelle say out the window, followed by a roar of laughter.

"Don't laugh," JT said. "It feels pretty good."

"I bet," Michelle snickered. "It doesn't look too bad, either . . . " followed by another round of uproarious chortling.

"Hey," she finally said after regaining her composure, "Charlie is up ahead. You guys might want to consider putting your clothes back on."

I suggested otherwise to JT. "This will be classic," I said to him. "Let's just run by Charlie as if nothing's out of place."

We eventually came upon Charlie and his pacer. It was very dark out, and before we knew it we were right behind them. We shuffled by nonchalantly. "Hey, Charlie," I said casually.

"Charlie?"

I turned back in horror. "Oh man . . . I'm so sorry . . . I thought you were Charlie Engle."

The two of them just stared at us queerly as we disappeared into the darkness. Eventually JT burst out in laughter. "As though that makes a difference," he roared.

"What do you mean?"

"You said to them, 'I thought you were Charlie Engle,' as though that made it okay for the two of us to be out here running naked."

"Well . . . didn't it?" I responded. This made him laugh even louder. We were two fools running naked through the night, and it was one of the most transformational experiences of my life.

• • • •

The rest of the race was horribly painful, but incredibly enriching. The struggle and hardship never went away, but now I savored and cherished it rather than battled it. Like life, running 135 miles across the desert was filled with pain and suffering. You either fought it the entire way, or accepted the fact of it and moved down the road harmoniously. I chose the latter path, and what a difference that made.

After crossing the finish line hand in hand with my crew, I informed them that I was going to drive back to Popou's house in Southern California.

"Karno," Michelle said, "I know you want to see your father, but you've been out here for a day and a half without sleep. It's probably not wise to drive right now. Let Popou get a few more hours of rest."

Of course, she was right. We spent the night at the Dow Villa in Lone Pine and left the next morning at 6:00.

When I got back to San Clemente and reached my parents' house, I rushed up the stairs and burst through the door. Popou was stretched out in an easy chair in front of the television watching (surprise, surprise!) golf. "Popou!" I ran over and hugged him.

"Hello, son." His voice was quiet, almost a whisper. "How'd it go?"

"Great. It was my worst result yet, but I've never had a better race. Enough about me, though. How the heck are you?"

"You know me," he whispered. "Never had a bad day."

That was the Popou I knew and loved! Here was a guy who could barely make it from his chair to the toilet and he was calling it a great day.

"Do you remember me talking to you in the recovery room after surgery?"

"No, I don't remember a thing. How'd I look?"

"Not good," I said. "About the same way you looked when you crewed for me at Badwater back in '96."

He wheezed and rocked back and forth. "Don't make me laugh." He grimaced. "It stretches my stitches."

I put my hand on his shoulder and chuckled. "I love you, Popou." And suddenly, the world was back in balance.

"Where's Yiayia?" I chortled. "We've got some celebrating to do!"

"Yes, we do," he said. "You guys have got to figure out a way to get me over to the golf course."

"*Opa* to that!" I said.

"Carpe diem!" he whispered in reply.

There will come a day when Popou can no longer swing a golf club, just as there will come a day when I can no longer run. But, thankfully, today is not that day. Opa!

7.0

Passing the Buck

"Run like you stole something."
—RED-HANDED RUNNER

THEY SAY A BUCK doesn't buy you much these days, though I beg to differ. I've found that a single dollar can be priceless. Let me explain why.

But first, please allow me to come clean. Okay, deep breath: I'm weird. Yes, I'm strange. There, I fessed up.

But when you think of it, who isn't? We all have our peculiar idiosyncrasies, don't we? Who among us can look themselves in the mirror and honestly say they're one hundred percent *normal*? Let's be candid: Being completely normal is, well, abnormal.

I hope you don't entirely disagree with this premise, so that when I tell you about a recent habit I've developed you won't think the asylum beckons. It all began one winter day near my home. I'd reached the midway point during an otherwise ho-hum training run, when I noticed a dollar bill blowing down the street. I picked it up. What good fortune, I thought. That dollar bill brought me a measure of happiness. On a scale of one to ten—one being utter misery and ten being supreme elation—I'll call it a seven.

Then I ran past a car with a flat tire. What lousy fortune, I thought. It troubled me that I'd just had good fortune bestowed upon me while the poor owner of this car had incurred just the opposite. It didn't seem fair. I wished that I could somehow share my good fortune with him to help offset his misfortune.

Then it occurred to me: Pass the buck. It might not cover the cost of replacing the tire, but it might lessen some of the emotional anguish. So I ran over to the car and tucked the dollar bill under the windshield wiper.

Guess what? That act also brought *me* a measure of happiness. In fact, using the same scale, it was pretty close to a perfect ten.

Wow, I thought, that was the most happiness a dollar bill has ever brought me. My tempo quickened, the sun burst through the clouds, and that ho-hum training run turned into a heart-pounding, adrenaline-filled sprint. Suddenly, my energy seemed boundless.

All for a buck!

That day marked a discovery. I discovered an innovative way to combine time spent training with goodwill.

Here's the lowdown. Before going for a run, I stuff a few dollar bills in my pocket. When I pass a random car, I place one under the windshield wiper. There's nothing scientific to it; I simply pick a car and stick a buck under the blade. I like to think whoever enters the car and finds that dollar bill neatly tucked against the windshield will be filled with a moment of joy.

The scenario I play in my mind is a young child, whose parents have been hit hard by the recession, discovering the dollar bill and saying, "Look, Mommy, even though the Tooth Fairy couldn't leave money under my pillow, she left it on our car instead!" Then the child smiles, revealing a missing tooth.

Of course, I also have visions of being tasered by some over-zealous meter maid, so I keep my new habit discreet. Better to maintain a low profile than risk receiving involuntary electroshock therapy from a 50,000-volt stun gun.

All right, so there you have it: I'm weird. Of course, there are worse vices I could have adopted, like plucking plastic bottles out of trashcans and depositing them in recycling bins. (Okay, I'm guilty of that one as well.)

My take is that when it comes to spreading good karma, no act is ever too small. Just look at the return on investment a buck can bring you.

I'd posted an entry on my *Runner's World* blog about this practice of placing dollar bills under the windshield wipers of parked cars. The column received an incredible response. Hundreds of readers left comments. One of them asked for my home address, which seemed odd. The brief exchanged that ensued went like this:

Me: Why do you want to know where I live?

Reader: So I can start parking my car in front of your house before your runs.

► Topher and crew at the finish of the Bay-to-Breakers race in San Francisco

8.0

Never Say Never

"Why, sometimes I've believed as many as
six impossible things before breakfast."

—QUEEN IN *THROUGH THE LOOKING-GLASS*

ONE COOL FALL morning in the hills above Silicon Valley,
something unexpected happened: Topher broke. For years he'd
watched from afar; he'd analyzed, he'd examined and studied, but
finally he just had to know for himself. On a whim, he ran eight
miles with me.

Good, I thought. Not just about the fact that he'd covered an
impressive distance for a first-timer, but also because of the impul-
sive nature in which he did so. One moment he'd never run a mile
in his life, the next he'd run for over an hour straight. This was
precisely the type of spontaneous abandonment one looks for in a
potential long-distance runner.

Researchers have shown that in certain susceptible individuals, a single "use event" can create an addiction. Granted, these studies pertain to nicotine, cocaine, heroin, alcohol, caffeine, and other addictive substances, but I have witnessed a similar phenomenon in certain runners, especially the good ones.

Next, Topher ran the annual Bay-to-Breakers race, a local favorite in the Bay Area. While it is not a particularly long race, the fact that he participated in a formal running event showed promise.

Then he purchased a pair of bona fide running shoes and started consistently running every single day without exception. This, I thought, was excellent. His obsessiveness was promising.

Thus, when he approached me after only a few short months of running and announced he wanted to enter a 50-K race, it didn't come as too much of a surprise. Still, fifty kilometers—thirty-one miles—is beyond a marathon. To go from never running in his life straight into an ultramarathon was either bold or foolish.

"Are you sure you want to start with an ultra?" I asked.

"Dude, it's only a few miles more than a marathon. Why not?"

I could think of a number of reasons why not, but I just bit my lip. I didn't want to stifle his fervor; then again, I didn't want to see him get injured. His legs were still pencil thin and his muscles underdeveloped. I was a bit concerned but figured, if nothing else, the results would be entertaining to watch unfold.

Indeed they were! Topher made the classic rookie mistake of letting his ego get the better of him during the early stages of the race. He paced himself appropriately for about the first hour— mixed somewhere near midpack of the racers—but then he gaffed. "I feel strong," he said to me. "Let's pick it up!"

Again I bit my lip, saying nothing and speeding up alongside him. This was a lesson best learned through experience. At least that's what the humanitarian side of me said. The devious side of me said it would be exceptional theater to watch his gradual demise. The moral split was about thirty/seventy.

To his credit, he maintained some semblance of composure for longer than what I'd predicted. With his more aggressive pace, he passed a lot of other runners and moved up considerably in the rankings. Clearly, this energized him, and he continued to push his pace. At mile twenty-seven, however, the proverbial wheels came off.

His tempo began to slacken, and now people began passing him. "What's up, Gaylord?" I chided. "Pick it up."

But there was no gas left in the tank. A 50-K ultramarathon is not about doing well for the first forty kilometers. It's not about having a great 45-K run. Unlike horseshoes and hand grenades, there is no "partial credit" received for getting close. An ultramarathon is about one thing and one thing only: crossing the finish line. He had to make it to fifty kilometers.

Actually, in this case, fifty-three kilometers. Apparently there wasn't a convenient place to stage the finish at the true 50-K mark, so the race directors added a slight extension. What's a couple extra kilometers among friends, right?

Wrong. Seems Topher didn't quite share this sentiment.

"What? You've got to be kidding me! We're not done?"

"Take it easy, little guy. It's not *too* much farther."

There is a colloquial saying in endurance racing that describes the action of catching and passing people along the course; it's said that you're "reeling them in." Well, let's just say we weren't the fishermen that day, we were the fish.

Nearly everyone we passed during the earlier stages of the race now returned the favor. So did most of those who had been behind us from the get-go. In fact, almost everyone in the entire field passed us. Topher had been rendered powerless. He hated being passed, but there was absolutely nothing he could do about it.

A sympathetic man would have offered his condolences. However, I am not a sympathetic man. Topher was defenseless, and such occurrences were indeed rare. Okay, priceless. I was determined to capitalize on the situation.

"Come on, Gaylord," I ribbed him. "I'd like to get there sometime this week." Ha! Ha! Ha! "You got weights or something attached to your shoes? Your feet are barely clearing the ground."

I should say that, in fair recognition of his efforts, he did demonstrate tremendous grit and determination in making it to the finish line that day. Either that, or his anger at my heckling propelled him onward.

Whatever the case, he made it, and though I would never admit to it, I was proud of him.

We convened for dinner that evening, Topher, Kim, Julie, and I, to celebrate Topher's accomplishment. His muscles were so tight he could barely make it from the car up the curbside. With a lot of moans and groans, he finally made it inside the restaurant.

At the end of dinner, he needed us to help get him out of his seat. "Ohhh . . . I'm so sore," he moaned.

"Just wait until tomorrow morning," I said.

"It's gonna get worse?"

"Just you wait." Then I added casually, "Of course, a vanduzzi could help."

"A what?"

"A vanduzzi. It's an ancient Greek remedy for alleviating muscle pain and stiffness. It pulls the toxins from your body."

This piqued his curiosity. "Where do I get one of these *vanduzzis*?"

"Funny you should ask. I could give you one. I'm quite good at it, actually. Used to give them to my dad all the time."

"How does it work, Karno?"

"It's hard to explain. Better to just get things set up."

A slight suspicion suffused his acceptance, but he was a desperate man and so he agreed to try it.

When we got back to their house, I pulled Kim aside. "Okay, Kimmy, I'm going to need a sturdy glass cup, some olive oil, a dollar coin, a swath of cloth, and a rubber band. Oh yeah, and some matches."

"Man, Karno," she said, "this sounds dangerous."

"Only for Topher." We both chuckled.

Topher was in the other room. "Okay, Toph, you'll need to lie flat on the couch. No, no, turn over, you'll need to be on your stomach." I wanted him on his stomach because I knew that if he saw the flame, he'd immediately bolt.

Reluctantly, he turned over. "Karno, are you sure you know what you're doing?"

"Trust me, I'm a pro."

Kim brought me the necessary supplies. I wrapped the piece of cloth around one side of the dollar coin and stretched it taut. I then wound the rubber band tight around the excess fabric on the other side to prevent the cloth from unfurling. Above the rubber band, I spread apart the cloth so that it resembled something of a budding flower.

The next step would require expert diplomacy. "Topher, I'm going to need you to pull down your pants."

Instantly, he protested. "What the . . . "

"You've got underwear on, right?"

"Well . . . yes. But . . . "

"They're not tighty whities, are they?"

"No . . . but . . . "

"Then you'll be fine. Everything's cool. Kimmy, help him get his pants down. For the vanduzzi to work properly, you need to apply it directly to the skin."

Topher was confused, thoroughly beat up, and completely exhausted, all elements that contributed to his extreme vulnerability. That was the key to pulling this off.

With his pants pulled down around his ankles, I swiftly rubbed a liberal coating of olive oil on the back of his upper leg.

"Karno! What are you doing?"

"Dude, chillax," I said calmly.

I took the excess olive oil left on my hand and rubbed it around the lip of the cup for added lubrication. Next, I placed the flat side of the coin in the middle of the area on his leg where I'd rubbed the oil.

When I lit the match, he freaked.

"What the f*#k!"

"Hold still!" I yelled. "We don't want anyone to catch fire here!"

He began screaming, "Kimmy! Kimmy! Help me!"

"Gaylord!" I yelled, "if you don't hold still, the entire house could go up in flames!"

He temporarily froze, and this gave me the opportunity I needed to light the cloth.

"I feel heat!" he roared.

"Good," I said, "that means it's working."

I motioned for the girls to come closer. "Watch this," I whispered.

Inverting the cup, I placed it over the top of the burning coin on the back of Topher's leg and pushed down forcefully.

"Ahhh!" he screamed.

The flame quickly began consuming all of the available oxygen in the cup, creating an incredibly powerful suction. As the air supply depleted, there was nothing left to draw in except Topher's skin.

The three of us watched in amazement as his flesh was sucked deeper and deeper into the cup, the olive oil assisting its passage.

Kim said, "Oh . . . my . . . God . . . "

Julie said, "Wouldja look at that . . . "

Topher yelled in horror. "What? What? What is it?"

The three of us admonished him to shut up and hold still. We didn't want anything wrecking our science project.

We stared, transfixed. The cup was nearly filled with Topher's skin. A smoldering coin and the charred remains of the burnt cloth rested on a small area at the top. The flesh inside the cup was deep purple in color, like that of a beet. We gazed in astonishment at the spectacle.

"Why is it that color?" Kim asked.

"Those are the toxins getting drawn up, the impurities being purged from his body," I said. I had absolutely no idea what I was talking about, but I spoke like a neurosurgeon.

"Get it off of me! Get it off of me!" Topher hollered.

"SHUT UP!" all three of us yelled. We were amazed.

Eventually, we'd had our fill. Getting the cup off was not going to be easy. The strength of the vacuum had created an incredibly powerful suction. Breaking that vapor lock would be no mean feat.

I turned to Julie and Kim. "Girls," I said, "you may not want to watch this."

Topher cried out, "What are you going to do? What are you going to do?"

I jumped on the couch and straddled his back with both knees, the front of my body facing his feet. Grabbing the cup firmly with both hands, I began to pull with all my might.

"Kimmy, get him off me!" Topher pleaded.

"Hold still, will ya. I'm only doing this to help."

"Yeah, Topher, stop wiggling so much. It's for your own good. Karno's only trying to help you," said Kim.

"Help me?" Topher choked. "He's trying to kill me!"

I wrung to the left, and then to the right, Topher's leg skin twisting as I did. But it was no use, the glass didn't budge. The cup stuck to his skin like an industrial-grade plunger.

"It's no use. We'll have to try something else." I needed to somehow break the seal. "Kimmy, do you have a rubber spatula?"

"Sure. It's in the kitchen. I'll get it."

"Rub some butter on it, will ya?"

She dashed off to the kitchen.

"What are you going to do now?!" Topher wailed.

"Relax, bud. We're gonna get that lamprey unstuck."

Kimmy returned with the spatula buttered and ready.

"Okay. When I pull up on the cup, wedge the corner of that spatula as far up into it as you can. We need to break the seal."

I torqued the cup while Kim jammed the spatula under one side. I pulled harder, the skin along Topher's entire upper leg lifting in response.

He screamed in agony.

Suddenly, the spatula ruptured the seal and the cup released with a loud "*POP!*" like the sound of a cork flying off a bottle of champagne. The discharge sent me tumbling backward.

Topher was screaming, but his shriek was temporarily muffled as I rolled over his head, pinning his face to the couch pillows. My momentum flipped me off the couch, and I landed on the floor.

I got to my knees and took quick inventory to make sure nobody was seriously injured.

Julie and Kim clapped approvingly. "Bravo! Well done!"

I stood up and bowed like a maestro, and the two girls patted me on the back. I was actually very pleased with the outcome. As far as vanduzzis go, it had been one of my finest.

Meanwhile, Toph lay on the couch moaning.

For the next several weeks, Topher's leg was straight out of *20,000 Leagues Under the Sea*. The welt on the back of his leg looked like a hickey from a giant squid. He tried concealing it by wearing longer shorts, but it was no use. Every time we went running, I'd slow down and jog behind him, so I could marvel at this massive conical hematoma. As much as he despised the purple welt, I found it a thing of beauty, a masterpiece, and proof of my skilled artistry as a vanduzzi* doctor.

Eventually, the swelling and discoloration faded, but not Topher's gusto. He continued running stronger than ever and set his sights on a fifty-miler not too far off.

• • • •

Can you imagine? He wanted to tackle a fifty-mile race after his less-than-pleasant experience during a 50-K. It was irrational. I loved it!

His running had become obsessive, fanatical, and reckless. In other words . . . *perfect*.

---

* Some of you might be wondering about the origins of the word "vanduzzi." To clarify its source, I must preface this explanation by describing a phenom-enon we affectionately refer to in my family as a "Popouism."

Basically, a Popouism is a host of idiosyncrasies exhibited solely by Popou, such as the tendency to get creative when applying the language arts in every-day use. As an example, while Yiayia's Greek is proper and eloquent, Popou's mastery of the Greek dialect is slightly less commanding. When speaking, if he arrives at a word he doesn't know or has forgotten the meaning of, he often gets, shall we say, inventive. More concisely, he often makes words up.

For instance, you don't peel an orange, you "fluvy" it. The insertion of Greek words while speaking English is nothing new in my family, and *most* of these words are legitimately Greek. You didn't pass gas in my family, you "broutsou'ed." You didn't sit on your ass, you sat on your "kolo." I remember going into a Kmart with my mom when I was a young boy and hearing some-one on the loudspeaker broadcast, "Paging Mr. Harry Kolo . . . Paging Mr. Harry Kolo." All the Greeks in the store started busting up. No one else had any idea what was going on.

The only difference with Popou is that he uses words that don't exist in *any* language. That, I believe, is the origin of words like "fluvy" and "vanduzzi." My best research has led me to the conclusion that the actual term for this practice is *Hijama* or cupping. This quasi-medical technique dates back to the days of Hippocrates, when physicians and healers employed the procedure to, as they put it, "Draw out and disperse stagnant and congested blood by using pathogenic heat to break up humors and bring toxins to the surface for release, thereby restoring flow of the Vital Force."

Whether all of that is true, I don't know. But one thing's for sure. When I plucked that cup off the back of Topher's leg, his reaction was so violent that I have to think I played some small role in reinvigorating his "Vital Force."

► Topher "Deer-in-the-Headlights" Gaylord and faithful partner, Kim

9.0

Seconds Matter

"Wherever you go, there you are."
—Buckaroo Banzai

OVER THE YEARS, I've had the honor of meeting many running greats like Carl Lewis, Frank Shorter, and Steve Scott. I recently sat on a panel with Deena Kastor, Josh Cox, and Ryan Hall, three of the world's premier marathoners. What strikes me as peculiar is the fact that while we're all runners, the events we compete in are almost entirely different sports.

These other runners' sports are all about speed. Whether it be the hundred-yard dash, the mile, or even the 26.2-mile marathon, they speak about maintaining blazing speeds. In discussing his third-place finish at the prestigious Boston Marathon, Ryan talked about "throwing down a 4:30 mile at the midway point."

A four-and-a-half-minute mile, I remember thinking to myself. That's insane! Then someone asked me about my second-place finish at the Sahara Race, a 155-mile ultramarathon across the blazing-hot Sahara Desert, and I talked about "throwing down a fifteen-minute-mile death slog in knee-deep sand with a twenty-five-pound pack on my back."

The crowd laughed, but I wasn't joking. The difference between the top finishers in a marathon can sometimes be just seconds. Can you imagine that, mere seconds separating racers after 26.2 miles? That's nuts! It's not unusual for top finishers in an ultramarathon to be separated by hours. Seconds don't matter. Who are they kidding?

• • • •

"Willie, are you sure we're going the right way?" Hilary asked.

"Trust me." It was dark and cold, but he spoke with an air of confidence.

"It's been over three hours since the last checkpoint." Until now, Hilary had never questioned anyone.

"We're right on track. I've been following the map precisely."

She let it go at that. As far as levelheadedness went, Hilary was the most composed individual I'd ever met, man or woman. I'd seen her pushed to the very brink before, and she'd never once lost her composure.

But this situation was getting more desperate with each passing minute. Once we'd climbed above 11,000 feet, the trail had become overgrown and completely indiscernible. It was 3:00 in the morning and the silvery moon cast off very little light. Compounding matters, it was bitter cold and mucky, our feet sinking knee-deep into the boggy sludge as we tried to maintain forward progress.

"You all right?" I asked Tim. He was one of the most seasoned among the four of us, but he had gone very quiet.

"I think so," he said. "My legs have gone numb, so I can't really tell."

An adventure racing team consists of a navigator (Willie), a female (Hilary), a captain (me), and the fittest, most experienced willing accomplice you can find (Tim). For the past forty-three sleepless hours we had been racing against other teams through the mountains of Utah. This was our second night without rest. We were currently in the lead—not that it mattered much right now. Survival had become our top priority.

As the team captain, it was up to me to make the tough executive decisions. I never doubted Willie's ability as a navigator. He was one of the most renowned mountain guides on earth and had ascended Mount Everest (the world's highest peak) on numerous occasions as well as pioneered routes up the side of Aconcagua (the highest peak in South America, where he was from).

But I was detecting a slight shift in Hilary's demeanor, so *I* did the talking this time.

"Willie, we're good, right?"

He was holding the laminated map in front of him and making careful observations as we moved.

"Trust me," was all he said. I was too tired and cold to argue.

Two hours passed. We were all miserable, soaked to the bone, sleep deprived, and very, very cold. But all four of us had been here before. This was the kind of adventure that defines individuals, shapes and molds character, separates the merely tough from the indomitable. It is what we live for. We pride ourselves on our ability to remain lucid during moments of great duress such as these.

But sometimes under such physical stress the mind can play tricks on you. Not this time.

"There it is!" Willie screamed.

By God, he was right. We had found the next checkpoint.

Supreme elation spread through the group as we began galloping toward the marker, trying to lift our legs high enough to clear the marshy surface swill. All was suddenly good.

The euphoria began to ebb slightly, however, when it appeared that something was strangely amiss. I couldn't quite put my finger on it at first, but the closer we got to the mark, it became increasingly apparent that something was wrong.

Suddenly, all wasn't so good. In fact, things were bad. Horribly bad. It was the same checkpoint we had been at five hours earlier. Essentially, we had been traveling in a huge circle for the past five hours.

Hilary absolutely lost it. In my wildest dreams, I never could have imagined her erupting with such fury. "Willie!" she screamed, "show me that map!"

Reluctantly, Willie held the map in front of her. She inspected it closely. Slowly, she raised her head and spoke.

"Willie," she said, "the map has been upside down!"

When Willie rotated the map into the upright position, with Hilary watching closely, we were able to eventually locate our current position and navigate to the next, and final, checkpoint of the race. When we reached this final transition before the finish, we were informed that our team was now in second place. While we had meandered in circles throughout the night, another team had passed us. It was a demoralizing pity to forfeit the top position after spending so many hours in the lead. We were deflated.

• • • •

The final discipline of this race was a mountain-biking segment. We'd passed the two-day mark and were all ready to reach the finish line. As the sun began rising, our team peddled along, seemingly content. But there was an undercurrent of disenchantment coursing through us now that we knew we were no longer going to win the race.

A long uphill climb remained. As we came around a sharp corner on the ascent, the first place team suddenly appeared. They were just ahead of us! And while we were tired and haggard, they looked *really* beat.

We rode assertively in a tight pack as we approached the leaders. Tim quietly issued a directive to our team: "When we pass them, show no signs of weakness. Look strong."

We did as he instructed and picked up the pace. When we reached them, they were clearly demoralized. "Well done," they said to us. "We thought you might catch us."

We congratulated them on their performance, but didn't slow down. When we crested the top of the climb, Willie checked the map and pronounced that the finish was just ahead.

We hooted and hollered as we tore down the road, flying downhill for the rest of the race and on to victory.

Then we heard the screaming. In our exuberance, we'd ridden right past the turn chute for the finish. "Stop!" one of the race marshals yelled over a loudspeaker. "Turn around!"

"We passed it, we passed it!" I shrieked. "Quick, everyone turn around."

Just as we spun around, though, the second place team crested the peak. Their eyes lit up when they saw our blunder. Suddenly, they were infused with crazy energy as they started racing down the slope.

We started racing back up to the turn for the finish, frantically retracing our path. They were coming down; we were peddling up. They reached the turn for the finish slightly before us.

The finish chute was perhaps a hundred yards—the length of a football field. All of us pedaled like maniacs: sweat flying, muscles stinging, dirt shooting in every direction. We were locked in a frenzied dash for the tape. Neck and neck we dueled, heads down, legs pumping, vision blurred.

Both teams burst across the finish line in an all-out sprint, fervently trying to edge out the other. What counted was the position of the fourth team member to cross the line. Theirs was a hair ahead of ours. After fifty hours of racing, we lost by a fraction of a second.

Seconds, I guess, do matter.

• • • •

Even though it was disappointing to finish in second place after putting forth such an all-out effort, some priceless nuggets of wisdom were gained along the way. These insights transcend athletics and extend to broader elements of life. Here are the four main takeaways.

1. It doesn't matter how fast you're going if you're moving in the wrong direction.

2. Even if you're inches away from the finish, never take success for granted.

3. Regardless of how distant your dreams may seem, every second counts.

4. Never, under any circumstances, argue with a tired woman. She is always right.

▶ Navigator Willie, "It's that way!"

10.0

Run for the Hills

"Adventure is just bad planning."

—ROALD AMUNDSEN

IN THE MOVIE *Crocodile Dundee*, the main character, an Australian tracker, is confronted by a trio of punks in a New York City alleyway, one of whom brandishes a switchblade. Dundee is advised by his American companion to hand over his wallet because the thief is wielding a knife. The Australian stares at the switchblade in curious amusement: "Knife? That's not a knife," he proclaims. Then he draws his massive bowie knife. "This is a knife!"

I love that scene because it illustrates the grandeur of the Australian spirit. Having lived there for a year as a high school exchange student, I know the bold, unpretentious Aussie nature well.

So perhaps I should have known better when I fielded a call from the folks at The North Face Down Under, inviting me to return to the enchanted land of wombats and wallabies, this time to do a little running.

"How far is the run?" I asked Wojo. (His given name is Daniel Wojciechowski, but the Aussies tend to truncate every word possible, a dialect they refer to as "Strine," which presumably stands for "Australian slang.")

"I dunno know how far it is. A few hundred kilometers, I guess." (To be precise, it's 570 kilometers—or about 350 miles—but who's counting?)

"How long will it take you?" he asked.

"That depends on the terrain. What's it like?"

"Oh, she's a beaut. PK and I Kombi'ed it. Tons of roo." Translation: *It is a beautiful course. Paul Karis and I drove a camper van along the route to scout it out. There are lots of kangaroos along the way.*

"Actually, Wojo, what I meant, is there much climbing and descending along the route?"

"From what I recall, not much. Maybe a couple hills."

Hills were of little concern to me; we have plenty of those in San Francisco. Given his report on the relatively mild terrain, I told him that I ought to be able to do it in six days.

It wasn't entirely clear what I was getting myself into, but sometimes you've just got to leap before you look. "The man who insists upon seeing with perfect clearness before he decides, never decides," Henri Frédéric Amiel once noted.

"Summit-to-Sydney," as they coined it, seemed straightforward: I would be running from the summit of Australia's highest mountain, Mount Kosciusko, to its biggest city, Sydney, a monumental and enchanting trek across the outback to the cultural epicenter of this island continent as a fundraiser for the Starlight Foundation. I couldn't wait!

The transpacific flight was a grunt. I don't sleep easily on airplanes, and I spent much of the journey pacing the aisle. No problem, I thought. I'll get some rest when I arrive.

Hardly. A flurry of nonstop activities ensued from the second I deplaned. I was starving by the time we loaded into the RV, dubbed the Mother Ship, for the long drive to Charlotte Pass. Joining us was a reporter from the Sydney *Sun-Herald*, Flip Byrnes, who would be documenting the endeavor for a feature story in an upcoming edition. I tried my best to be conversational, but the ride was bumpy and nauseating. Jet-lagged and exhausted as I was, all I wanted to do was curl up and sleep somewhere.

After a long night, we arrived at our destination, which I quickly realized was not the summit of Mount Kosciusko but a parking lot some ten kilometers below. The crew explained that we couldn't get any closer on the paved road so I'd have to run to the summit. Yes, the climb was steep, but they assured me it's all downhill from here.

So off I went scurrying up Mount Kosciusko. A couple of hours later, after scaling this little "hill," I returned to the parking lot where my run to Sydney began in earnest.

The first day of running wasn't exactly *all* downhill. Yes, there was an overall net loss of elevation, but there were plenty of undulations along the way. Basically, I was climbing or descending the entire day.

The sunset, however, made up for the anguish. It was one of the most brilliant I'd ever seen. The air was amazingly clear, dry, and motionless. Huge gum trees shrouded the western skyline, the silhouette of each drooping branch distinct under the burning red sun that shone in the distant horizon. Beyond the periodic cry of a magpie or a kookaburra, there was only ear-ringing silence.

I ran alone in the warm twilight. Somewhere ahead in the distance, the Mother Ship peacefully motored along. We were the sole humans on this remote byway. Stars appeared above, at first dim and then dazzling. The Southern Cross emerged in the infinite cosmos like a honing beacon, Alpha and Beta Centauri radiating through the darkness. Although I felt at home, the foreign constellations reminded me that I was a long way from it.

• • • •

My Aussie crew knew how to do things right. They had hired a professional chef to prepare our meals, and he stocked the refrigerator with "heaps" of provisions: green shallots, fresh heads of lettuce, vine-ripe tomatoes, robust sweet onions. Of course, being true countrymen, the refrigerator was also well supplied with Fosters (i.e., Aussie beer).

When I arrived at the Mother Ship, the chef opened the refrigerator door to begin preparation. A slurry of rotting vegetables, beer, and melted butter came pouring out, quickly coating the floor and saturating the shag carpet of the RV. The cooling system had broken during the bumpy drive, breaking the beer bottles and wreaking havoc on the cooler's contents, which had baked in the midday sun. The Mother Ship stank.

"No worries," Wojo proclaimed. "She'll be right, mate."

I was tired, hungry, and cold. I wanted nothing more than a

warm, home-cooked meal, but it was not to be. I climbed into my bunk with a solitary banana for dinner. There was a smile on my face, however. No matter how dismal things appeared at the moment, it didn't matter. The stars shined brightly above, and miles of wild, open countryside stretched before us. Wojo's words rang true: She'll be right . . .

In the morning, a herd of kangaroos and wombats gathered outside the camper in the predawn cool. Cute little buggers, PK put it. All seemed right . . . until I began the run.

The second day of running was no less strenuous than the first. The terrain in between the remote outback towns was much more difficult than what I'd anticipated. Rarely was there a flat section that I could just cruise. I seemed to be climbing and descending endlessly.

"Man, I'm beat," I groaned to Wojo. "I've been running up the Hyde Street hill [the notoriously steep three-hundred-foot rise the cable cars scale in San Francisco] to train, but this is killing me."

He looked at me incredulously. "Hill? That's not a hill," he said, turning to face the monster before us. "*This* is a hill."

In front of us stood a 3,300-foot *hill,* the equivalent of eleven Hyde Streets stacked one upon the other.

Nice.

Over the next several days, we crisscrossed the Great Australian Dividing Range, climbing and descending some 30,000 feet in total. Little "hills," I guess, in these parts.

To my amazement and delight, the crew rose to the occasion. Each of them took turns running with me at various points, even the chef, who claimed not to be a runner (unless there was an Aussie rules football and Fosters involved).

In her story, Flip quoted my comments on Wojo completing a forty-eight-kilometer stretch beside me. "That's inspiring," I said, "when you see someone hurting more than you."

Wanting an immersive experience, Flip even joined the procession. She penned, "The sun beats down and I jump in for a run. Karnazes greets me with a smile and a friendly 'Hi, ma'am.'"

Later in the story, she captured an archetypal Aussie understatement: "North Face general manager and mastermind of the Kosciusko run, Paul 'PK' Karis, says tomorrow will be the crux of the race. 'There will be more hills. Lots of hills. In the Tour de France, this would be the Pyrenees. Races are made and lost on the hill stage.'"

Earth to PK: If I'm not mistaken, the Pyrenees are referred to as the *mountain stage*.

Supportive as the crew was, the days began to melt together. The run was punishing. Back-to-back sixty-mile days wore on me, physically and emotionally. Sydney seemed galaxies away.

The crew sensed my exhaustion. They saw hopelessness in my eyes at times. Flip, though, remained optimistic. As we climbed yet another foreboding rise in the Great Divide, we emerged upon an iconic bush town. A broad smile cracked my face. Later, Flip would write that I was "still chipper." She described the pub at Nerriga emptying as we passed. "Six people gripping beers cheer him on."

I felt enlivened by the people rooting for me out in the middle of nowhere, their camaraderie and enthusiasm awakening my fighting spirit and making me stronger. After passing through the booming metropolis of Nerriga, we were back in "woop woop" (Strine for the "middle of nowhere").

Chef continued to baffle us all with his uncanny ability to create culinary masterpieces out of thin air. Our early dinner that night was no exception. I came running around a corner in the road and there, on the gravel roadside, was a complete spread of steaming Asian food laid out on a linen-covered table (the Aussies brought a portable table, linen tablecloths, china dishware, silver utensils, and crystal goblets; the latter for their beer, of course). It was a gourmet meal, elegantly presented on a desolate red dirt road miles from anything.

As much as I wanted to sit and enjoy the buffet, I still had much distance left to cover. So I piled a heaping serving of the stir-fried vegetables and roasted shrimp on my china plate, grabbed a shiny silver fork, tucked a linen "serviette" in my running shorts, and bade farewell to the crew. Off I went running down the road, eating as I jogged.

We hadn't seen another vehicle in hours when I heard the distant rumble of a car slowly approaching. Mostly I could hear the clanking of its rickety suspension on the bumpy dirt road. The car wasn't going fast, just cruising along casually on the dusty pathway, but everything rattled.

As it emerged from behind a tree-lined bend in the road, I saw that it wasn't a car at all, but a late-model pickup truck. As the vehicle passed, I nodded at the occupants in between bites.

What I saw next, I'll never forget. Behind the wheel was an old Australian rancher clad in overalls. Beside him sat his old Australian shepherd. The look they gave me was as though they'd seen a space alien. The rancher's head rotated 180 degrees as he slowly drove by, transfixed on this otherworldly Martian running alongside the road while dining pleasantly. As his head spun, so did the shepherd's in perfect unison.

He'd probably driven this road for the past forty years without seeing a solitary soul. Today, a man in brightly colored gear eating a plate of freshly prepared gourmet food from a china plate strode by. *What was the world coming to?* he probably wondered.

Sunrise the next morning brought a renewed sense of optimism. We were getting nearer to the coastline with each passing day and the air felt thicker and rejuvenating. Flip wrote, "It's now day five, the bulk of the hills are behind him, and the road is now paved. Karnazes easily completes forty-two kilometers—a marathon—before noon. Yesterday he had to dig really deep. He ran 9,900 feet of ascent and about 12,000 feet of descent. It is dark when he cruises into Shellharbour, having notched up one hundred kilometers in a day. 'Today was great. I feel great,' Karnazes said cheerfully."

Flip seemed amazed that I was able to reconstitute on day five the way I had. She wanted to know how I managed to push through the darkness and moments of desolation experienced during the earlier stages of the run. I explained to her that I trained my body and mind diligently. I relentlessly condition and prepare, and then I asked a lot of my body in return. I try to make the very best out of what I've got; which, personally, I don't think is a whole heck of a lot. I'm not a special guy, I told her. I am not gifted.

Never, however, do I take shortcuts. There is no path of least resistance in my training. What I do equates to hard manual labor, disciplined grunt work. Once you permit yourself to compromise, you fail yourself. You might be able to fool some people, but you can never fool yourself. Your toughest critic is the one you face every morning in the mirror.

I'm far from great, I told her, "But if you're passionate and driven, you can accomplish things."

Apparently Flip felt inspired. She is going to run a marathon, she tells me. My only hope is that she still likes me when it's over.

Things got easier from that point forward. Other runners found me along the roadside and joined me. At first it was just a handful of folks. Later, as we neared Sydney, entire running clubs joined me. People made generous donations to the Starlight Foundation, contributing over ten thousand dollars when all was said and done.

The final stretch was a cordoned-off byway down a main street in Sydney. Where days earlier I had been running alone through the remote bush, I was now moving through the bustling shopping mecca of Pitt Street with hundreds of runners by my side and thousands of onlookers watching as we strode past.

We finished at The North Face flagship retail store and toasted not with champagne, but with Fosters. Six days and 570 kilometers after beginning this endeavor, we had made it. The Mother Ship would forever reek of fermented vegetables and warm beer, but the nightly aroma had become endearing; I would miss it.

After I showered, they whisked me off to the airport. I was heading to Japan for an ultramarathon three days later. On the drive, I penned a quick thank-you note to my Aussie team, which Flip quoted in the article she published in the *Sun Herald:*

For the support crew, all newly addicted runners, he leaves a note: Should we ever want to go for a long run, he knows this really great route from the highest peak to Australia's largest city. "There are a couple little 'hills' involved, but it's worth every step," says the Ultramarathon Man.

►PK, Wojo, Karno, Tinks, and Chef

11.0

Dreadville

"Fall seven times, stand up eight."
—JAPANESE PROVERB

"YOU DON'T EVEN look tired," I remember one of my support crew members saying to me at the Twin Lakes aid station. I was having a good race.

Runners pass through Twin Lakes twice during the Leadville Trail 100-Mile Run, the first pass at mile thirty-eight on the way out to the turnaround point at the halfway mark, and then again at mile sixty-one on the way back to the finish. I was on the return journey.

"Thanks," I told him, "I feel great." Then I set out toward the finish line.

My sights were now set on a top ten placing, maybe even top five. Word was that many of the runners in front of me looked haggard. Not me. I was going strong. Off I dashed down the trail, in the hunt, as they say, looking for runners in front of me to overtake.

The air was warm and calm as I wove my way along the tree-lined trail through the Colorado Rockies. People had warned me about the altitude, saying that it could sneak up on you unexpect-edly. After all, the Leadville Trail 100-Mile Run is coined "the Race Across the Sky." I wasn't concerned. I'd already climbed and descended Hope Pass twice, elevation 12,526 feet, and was handling the elevation just fine. Besides, I had done this same thing before—flown in from sea level the day prior to a mountain race—and fared just fine, placing top ten at a race that was reportedly tougher than this one, the Wasatch Front 100, even after going in the wrong direction for an hour in the middle of the night.

The fishing was good today. I began reeling in runner after runner. It's not that I was moving so swiftly, it's that they were mov-ing so slowly.

Things looked bright as I steadily moved up through the ranks. The next aid station, Half Moon, was nine miles beyond Twin Lakes, and I was certain I'd be coming up on it shortly. My pace quickened. Who knew how many more people I'd pass between here and the finish line?

My last semicoherent thought was that the trail had turned into molten glass. Suddenly, my legs were Jell-O. In the space of less than thirty feet, I'd gone from charging along to wobbly, barely able to place one foot in front of the other. My steps became delib-erate and calculated, requiring concentration just to lift my feet off the ground.

Now the same runners I had passed earlier began passing me, along with a cadre of others. The tables had been turned; it was I who was now being reeled in.

Sometimes you're a fisherman, and sometimes you're a fish.

I have no recollection of being escorted into the medic tent. All I recall is lying flat on my back on a cot while having a quasi-sobriety test administered.

The medic held up three fingers. "How many fingers do I have up?" he asked.

Well, that was a stupid question. Any child could tell he was holding up three fingers. What kind of foolish games were they playing? But I couldn't answer his question.

I tried to say the words, but nothing came out. I knew in my mind that he was holding up three fingers, though I couldn't formulate an answer.

Then he held up four fingers. "How many fingers now?"

More mockery. What an easy answer.

But, again, I couldn't articulate a response. I could plainly see four fingers, but something wasn't processing in the place in my brain where I was supposed to formulate the words.

Events transpired in a weird time warp from there. My crew appeared in the tent. I heard reference to HACE (high altitude cerebral edema). The medic instructed my crew that they needed to drive me down to Denver and lower altitude immediately. Then came voices, commotion, the sound of car doors slamming. The interior was dark. The vehicle lunged from side to side. I lay across the backseat. Time went by. How much time, I did not know. The sun was rising. I was in a hospital bed. No, wait, this was a hotel bed. My body felt clammy, though I wasn't cold. I lay motionless, except for my eyeballs scanning the sparsely decorated room.

Leadville had kicked my ass, and it was glorious. Failure rocks!

• • • •

Over the years, I've come to not only embrace failure, but to welcome it and celebrate the occurrence. You cannot grow and expand your capabilities to their limits without running the risk of failure. And failure can provide invaluable lessons.

Leadville taught me that past performance is no guarantee of future success. I had acted with reckless arrogance and paid the price. Just because I performed well in the Wasatch mountain range at a previous high-altitude race without training didn't necessarily mean that I would fare equally well in future forays. On my next assault of Leadville I would travel to Colorado well in advance of the race to give my body proper time to acclimatize. Nothing would be left to chance. For round two, I would be adequately prepared. This time, it would be me who was doing the fishing.

It worked. Arriving in the mountains a week prior to the race, my body had adapted to the elevation. I made it through mile seventy and then mile eighty. Everything was going as planned.

That is, until a concealed tree root caught the toe of my shoe and sent me flying. As my body hurtled forward, the root held my leg back and hyperextended my knee. Sitting in the dirt on the trailside, I flexed my leg several times. But doing so was excruciatingly painful. My knee made a creaking noise when I moved it. Not good.

Making the decision to withdraw was painful. My pledge has always been to never give up unless I am at risk of doing lasting or permanent damage to my body. Such was the case with my second failed attempt at Leadville.

The pain of not finishing this event cut deeper than the stinging in my knee, however. I had invested so much time and energy toward the completion of this event, and now all was lost.

UCSF Medical Center is renowned for its orthopedic surgery department. The doctor I was scheduled to see came highly recommended as a sports specialist. After all, he was the team physician for the San Francisco 49ers football squad.

When I entered his office, he took one look at me and said, "You're a runner, you're going to have horrible knees."

After seeing me and taking some X-rays, he informed me that I had a torn meniscus. He gave me some pills and told me to stop running. He instructed me to schedule a follow-up appointment in two weeks. I walked out of his office, threw the drugs in the trashcan, and went running.

I never returned.

• • • •

Years passed and Leadville weighed heavy on my mind. The media and press coverage that I was beginning to garner always focused on my successes. When I tried to point out my failures, no one seemed interested. I wanted people to know that I didn't always succeed, but that part of my story rarely got told.

Eventually, another opportunity arose for me to seek redemption at Leadville. On this occasion, the training and preparation would be extensive, perhaps too much so. I'd set my sights on the quest of running fifty marathons, in fifty states, on fifty consecutive days. In preparation for the undertaking, I'd embarked on an aggressive training program to condition my body for the rigors of this unique challenge. Part of the plan included running a number of hundred-mile races leading up to the mega-marathon attempt, the logic being that if I could comfortably run a hundred-mile race, running fifty consecutive 26.2-mile races might actually be doable.

But Leadville had always been anything but comfortable. While I'd handily completed many other hundred-milers, Leadville had repeatedly vexed me. I was scheduled to run three hundred-milers in the two months prior to Leadville and feared that I might not be adequately recovered. Still, I wasn't about to pass up this opportunity to try.

My trusted friend Martin Franklin volunteered to pace me during the final stages of the race. An Ironman and accomplished endurance athlete, Martin lived in Colorado, though he traveled extensively because of his work. So he was accustomed to the toll that shifting from sea level to high altitude without sufficient acclimatization could take on the body. One of the brightest people I knew, Martin would have all types of sophisticated strategies for overcoming altitude sickness, I was sure.

The third attempt at the Leadville Trail 100-Mile Run started well enough, but halfway up Hope Pass things went to pieces. An acidic nausea ravaged my guts and left a gritty, foul taste in my mouth, as though I were sucking on rusty nails. I slowed my pace, going into death-march gear in hopes of groveling my way to the top. The situation appeared bleak. If I somehow made it to the summit, I would have to drop down the backside, hit the turn-around point, and then reclimb the beast that was Hope Pass from the backside once again. I put my head down and placed one weary foot in front of the other, hoping for the best and unwilling to quit.

Somehow, I made it over the peak. Weaving my way down the backside, I tried to make a mental note of the terrain I would have to cover on my return. After an hour of running downhill as fast as I could, I stopped keeping track. It was too demoralizing. The thought of retracing those steps on a climb back up crushed me.

On my ascent up the backside of Hope Pass, my ears rang and my vision blurred, but dammit, I wasn't giving up! The idea of stopping seemed more permanently damaging than the risk of carrying on.

It started to hail. Great. Let the heavens part and thunder and lightning rain down upon me, I wasn't stopping. There was no logic in my approach at this point; I was beyond realizing my incoherence. This was a dangerous place to be, but I was too far gone to recognize it.

I'm not sure how I made it back over Hope Pass a second time. I'd like to claim that it was a calculated strategy that pushed me skyward, but in reality it was something more akin to mindless tenacity: I just kept putting one foot in front of the other, thoughtlessly determined, running the risk of imploding with each stride but impervious to good judgment and unwilling to stop. As Winston Churchill advised, "If you are going through hell, keep going."

When Martin found me on the trail at mile seventy-seven, he could tell something was wrong. His first clue: I was carrying a bouquet of wildflowers. Apparently I'd been picking them from the trailside as I ran.

We took off together trying to complete the last twenty-three miles of the race. Bless the man. Here was a highly accomplished entrepreneur and athlete patiently nurturing a bumbling idiot through the Colorado wilderness in the middle of the night. The fact that he volunteered to escort me on this endeavor speaks volumes about his character.

If things had been bad in the earlier stages of the run, they became even worse in the later stages. The nausea finally got the better of me. I pulled off the trail, opened my jaw, and began ejecting the contents of my guts forcefully, the beam from my headlight illuminating the streaming gush.

Martin stood nearby, listening and watching. "That's good," he said. "Get it all out." When the eruptions finally subsided, he offered some water. I took a swig, swished it around in my mouth, and spit it out.

"Let's go," I said. The stench was too much for me to bear.

We ran for about ten miles together through the darkness, exchanging hardly a word. A lot of fun I was on a Saturday night. We wove alongside Turquoise Lake in an endless succession of twists and jags, trying to avoid low-hanging tree branches and slippery rocks. As I stepped on one particularly slick rock, my leg slid out sideways from underneath me, and I came crashing down on the hard surface with a thud. I landed on my hip and elbow. The pain of impact instantly elicited another round of vomiting.

Lying there on my side, next to a puddle of puke, I wanted to curl up into a ball and evaporate. There were so many thoughts and scenarios racing through my mind: If I didn't make it, who would retrieve me from the trail? How would Martin get home? What should I do about the nausea? How was I going to contact my family? There seemed to be a staggering assortment of decisions to be made, and I was paralyzed by the complexity of it all.

"Martin," I whispered, "what should I do?"

I'm not sure if he could sense my inner turmoil, but his response was profound: "Simple," he said. "You've got a single choice to make: You either stop or you continue."

That was it. No superfluous complications, no unwarranted ponderings, no unnecessary analysis. Just one straightforward choice: Stop or go.

Put in those stark terms, the choice was crystal clear. "Onward!" I proclaimed defiantly.

His simple words juiced me with adrenaline. They stretched beyond running into every element of life. When situations seem thorny and convoluted beyond reconciliation, the weight of the complexities often blurs the simple reality that there is really only one fundamental decision to be made: Stop or continue. I decided to continue and suddenly I had an unflinching sense of purpose.

Like most other ultra trail races, the prize for finishing the Leadville Trail 100-Mile Run is a belt buckle (the genesis of these events was an endurance horse race, and they've kept the theme). But the Leadville buckle is unique. A honking mass of oversized metal, it is bigger than life, as much of a mantle piece as anything you'd wear around your waist.

Traditionally, there are two types of belt buckles that can be earned during these races: one for completing the grueling course in under the official cutoff time (which is typically thirty to thirty-two hours), and another for completing the race in under twenty-four hours. The prize for finishing within the latter at the Leadville Trail 100-Mile Run is a beautifully ornate, handcrafted silver buckle. It is one of the most prized possessions there is in ultra trail running.

"Martin," I puffed, "do you think we can get to the finish in under twenty-four hours?"

He looked at his watch. "That's a question for you. Personally, I think the answer is yes."

He believed. And so did I.

We tore off into the darkness with a renewed sense of vigor. The fear of failure was no longer in my mind. The only way I could fail was to give up trying, and that wasn't going to happen.

Not wanting to leave anything to chance, Martin drove me relentlessly. We had built up a bit of a buffer on the twenty-four-hour mark, yet we both knew things could deteriorate quickly and without warning. Maintaining a sub-twenty-four-hour pace was killing me, and the very real danger was that I would jeopardize finishing (at all) in pursuit of the elusive silver buckle. "Bucklemania" had snatched the spoils of victory from many a runner. I was smarter than that. Or so I thought.

My legs became wobbly and my vision grew increasingly cloudy, even though I have twenty/twenty eyesight. Distances blurred and even familiar nearby objects, like trees, began losing their distinguishing features. Individual branches took on the appearance of one conical blob.

Bucklemania or not, however, it was full speed ahead.

Thankfully, we made it! Martin had taken a calculated risk in pushing me so hard, and his intuition was spot on.

The final stretch of the course passes through the main street of the small township of Leadville. When I saw the finish tape in the distance, the clouds in my eyes disappeared. I began sprinting up the road, buoyed by the sense that I'd poured every single molecule of my being into crossing that line.

We bounded across the finish in twenty-three hours and twenty-four minutes. Merilee, the race director, gave me a big hug and congratulated me on a strong finish. I told her that it had required tremendous pain and suffering to make it here in under the twenty-four-hour mark.

"Why twenty-four hours?" she asked.

"For the silver buckle," I responded, surprised by her question.

"Oh, you didn't realize?"

"Realize what?"

"You have twenty-five hours at Leadville."

Doh! In all my attempts at Leadville, I had been so focused on just finishing the darned thing that I had failed to recognize they give you an extra hour.

And so ended my quest to complete the Race Across the Sky. It was the perfect ending to a noteworthy chapter in my running career. My final finishing result was respectable, though far from spectacular. But the sense of accomplishment was supreme. The month prior I had won the Vermont 100 Endurance Race, but that victory came without much struggle. Even though I won, I didn't feel as though I had given it my all. Leadville was just the opposite, and the gratification was much deeper.

We often think people who achieve great things never fail, that success comes naturally to them. This, of course, is a mistake. Truth is that risk-taking breeds failure and failure breeds success.

Basketball legend Michael Jordan said it perfectly: "I've missed more than nine thousand shots in my career. I've lost almost three hundred games. Twenty-six times, I've been trusted to take the game-winning shot and missed. I've failed over and over and over again in my life. And that is why I succeed."

It has been said that no success or failure is necessarily permanent. But I now own a Leadville Trail 100-Mile Run silver buckle, and that *is* permanent. What did I do with this prized possession? I put it in a box in my garage with all my other belt buckles, trophies, and awards. In the end, the physical piece of metal hardly means anything to me. What matters is the experience and accomplishment that I will carry in my heart and spirit for the rest of my life.

Get After It

"Not everyone who chased the zebra caught it, but he who caught it, chased it."

—SOUTH AFRICAN PROVERB

NOT ONLY DID Topher finish his first fifty-miler, he excelled. More importantly, he thrived on the experience. The incongruous magic of long-distance running was now in his blood, and he thirsted for more.

So when he told me he wanted to attempt the Western States 100-Mile Endurance Run, it came as little surprise. If he had informed me of this same thing eight months prior, I would have laughed. But now I knew he was serious.

Qualifying for Western States, however, is no walk in the park. Like the Boston Marathon, Western States only accepts the most elite (i.e., the *real* nuts). The qualifying standard is to complete a fifty-mile run in fewer than eleven hours. Topher had finished his first fifty-mile race within this standard.

However, running one hundred miles nonstop is not twice as demanding as running fifty miles; it's four or five times more difficult. Topher began increasing his weekly mileage in preparation for the challenge. And he began experiencing something familiar to many runners: injuries.

They weren't major injuries, but nagging discomforts that he'd never in his life experienced. Basically, pain. Lots of it, resulting from lovely little things like shin splints, neuromas, and an alarming condition where the bones along the front of his legs became spongy, yielding to firm finger pressure like a piece of moderately ripe fruit.

He called me one afternoon from his office. "What's happening to me, Karno?"

"I think you're turning into a melon."

"Ha, ha . . . very funny. Seriously, what do you think I should do?'

"I think you should run farther."

"Are you kidding?"

"Look, Topher, I'm flattered that you would ask me, but I'm probably the last guy you want to take advice from."

He kept running. Minor aches and pains have a way of working themselves out. The body adapts. As Topher's running progressed, his physical transformation was shocking. Those once beanpole legs of his took root and grew into gnarled, powerful appendages capable of propelling his body up tall mountains. The metamorphosis was startling, like those cheesy before-and-after photos in weight-lifting magazines advertising miracle muscle-bulking potions.

With our good friend Jim Vernon, the three of us started training on a regular basis. Jim was an accomplished athlete in his own right. He'd run the same 50-K and fifty-mile races as Topher and had also qualified for Western States. Jim was new to ultramarathoning, but no stranger to madcap adventure. We'd once spent two days wandering through the wilderness of the Trinity Alps with limited provisions in search of a supposed outpost with supplies and equipment. We later learned that the area we passed through was notorious for aggressive bears.

Both Jim and Topher worked at the outdoor clothing and gear company The North Face, and during Monday morning staff meetings they would commiserate about their residual ailments resulting from the weekend's activities. For both of them, this was a journey into uncharted waters, the frontier of self-potential. They were learning a lot about the trails throughout the Bay Area, but they were learning more about themselves. As Sir Edmund Hillary noted, "It's not the mountain we conquer, but ourselves." Adventure happens within.

While Topher's training progressed nicely, I thought the one element he might be lacking was the experience of running all night. Many of the racers at Western States would spend the entire night traversing the trails, and running at 3:00 A.M. is an entirely different experience than running at noon.

So I designed a course that would lead us on an all-night foray and invited Topher to join me. I told him the route I had conceived would encompass the best of both worlds.

"What does that mean?" he asked.

"Let's just say we'll encounter several types of wildlife along the way." I told him to meet me at my house at 10:00 on Friday night.

When Friday rolled around, I loaded my pack with provisions, put fresh batteries in my headlamp, and filled the internal bladder of my pack with electrolyte fluid. We left my house in the lower Pacific Heights district of San Francisco as scheduled and headed toward Fisherman's Wharf. The route we'd follow was designed to engage the senses and showcase some of the best locations the Bay Area had to offer. Perhaps some of the worst, too.

First we encountered the huge steaming cauldrons of crabs cooking along the street as we passed through Fisherman's Wharf. Massive plumes of mist rose into the night and filled the air with the scents and smells of boiling seafood and fresh-baked sourdough bread.

From there we headed up Powell Street, famous for the cable car line that runs along it. Powell is a steep climb, and we raced a cable car for a few blocks before nearly passing out from exhaustion. The passengers didn't quite know what to make of us at first, then they started yelling encouragement, urging us not to give up until we got to the top of the hill. Of course, they were all riding a cable car. None of them volunteered to hop off and run with us.

At the crest of the hill is the intersection with Lombard Street, known widely as "the Crookedest Street in the World." We ran down it.

This deposited us in the Italian enclave of North Beach. We ran past the famous Stinking Rose restaurant, and the scent of garlic was so thick it hung on your clothing. The only odor more asphyxiating came farther down the street where we encountered a group of old Italian men sitting at a roadside café toking huge cigars in between shots of grappa. They laughed at us as we ran by.

We jokingly coughed and choked as we jogged. They laughed harder. We loved it. So did they. Viva Italia!

Another San Francisco hill rose before us, this one up to one of the city's most iconic beacons, the Coit Tower. A 210-foot-high Art Deco tower, it rests majestically atop Telegraph Hill and offers sweeping views of San Francisco Bay and Alcatraz Island. As we reached the tower, the lights along the waterfront sparkled on the bay. I turned to Topher and asked, "Shall we kiss?"

He squinted at me. "Touch me and I'll kill you."

"But this is the city of love."

"I mean it, bro. Get anywhere friggin' close to me and you die."

So much for the liberal, free-thinking San Franciscans we pretended to be.

From there we headed toward the dark side of town, SoMa. Known for its collection of eclectic bars and pulsing nightlife, the South of Market area of San Francisco was jumping with activity. We ran past Hamburger Mary's, a popular late-night outpost catering to the least discriminating of palates (i.e., the *really* drunk), and then past the Holy Cow nightclub, where a life-sized Jesus Christ cow emblazoned with a tattooed peace sign dangled from above the entrance.

The revelers along the streets hooted and yelled at us as we ran by. "Out for a marathon?" one of them jeered. "Whaddaya running from?" another heckled.

"Toph," I said, stopping him, "we've gotta have a celebratory shot."

"Of what?"

"Bad tequila, of course. It's what got me running."

"Dude, there's no way I'm drinking bad tequila. Now, good tequila, that's a different story."

We headed into the nearest bar and ordered two shots of Patrón Platinum.

With the cockles warmed (actually, superheated), we took off toward the Tenderloin, a district many avoid at all costs. I thought running through the Tenderloin at midnight could actually be quite entertaining—if we didn't get shot.

We first came across a transvestite hooker standing on the corner with his (or her?) pimp. Lovely.

"Why are we going this way?" Topher said uneasily.

"Just shut up and run," I instructed.

We passed pushers doing deals in dark alleys, winos vomiting on the sidewalk, prostitutes parading their "assets" along the street, and Rastafarians freely partaking in the burning of their sacred herb. Oh, how I loved this city!

Topher looked terrified; I'd never seen him run so fast.

Once we'd survived the Tenderloin, it was out to the waterfront and west to the Golden Gate Bridge. We were now in a less-populated area and could relax a bit and just enjoy the surroundings. It was an absolutely stellar night: A whimsical fog swept into the middle of the bay like a river of fluffy cotton.

When we reached the south side of the Golden Gate Bridge, I explained to Toph a little game we'd need to play to get across. They close the sidewalk to pedestrians at night, so we had no choice but to take matters into our own hands.

"After we hop the fence and start running, you're going to

hear some commands coming over the loudspeaker. Don't pay attention to them."

"What will they be saying?" he asked.

"STOP, OR YOU'LL BE ARRESTED," I said.

"Hell no! I'm not going."

"It's cool. All we need to do is make it to the halfway point. They'll let us go after that."

"And what if we don't make it that far?"

"They'll arrest us. So run fast."

We hopped the fence. Just as we did, sure enough the loudspeaker blared. Topher did as I had instructed. He started sprinting like a scared rabbit. It was all I could do to keep up with him.

The bridge patrol must have found us more of an amusement than a threat because they didn't even bother to send a patrol car after us. Either that, or they were just too sleepy to care. After all, it was approaching 2:00 A.M., and this was a pre-9/11 world. The watch over national treasures like the Golden Gate Bridge was less heightened then. We were just two nutcase late-night runners out practicing our lunacy.

Once we made it across the bridge, the path was a familiar one. We headed up Conzelman Road to the top of the headlands. The view from the summit offered a 360-degree sweeping panoramic of the Bay Area. Even though it was the middle of the night, you could see all the way down the peninsula, the lights of Silicon Valley illuminating the distant sky.

"Karno, how 'bout that kiss now?"

"Get away from me, you freak!"

"I thought you were a liberal, freethinking San Franciscan."

"You thought wrong. Get anywhere friggin' close to me and you die."

With our headlamps switched on, we headed down the road to Coastal Trail, then proceeded through Tennessee Valley and out to Muir Beach, climbing and descending several significant peaks along the way. The sound of waves crashing along the shoreline ruled the night. There was a big northwest swell running and the ground trembled.

"Surf's gonna be good tomorrow. We should hit it."

"Karno, I'm not even sure I'll be alive tomorrow. Let's just get through tonight."

"Save your legs, bro. The best has yet to come."

"Dude, wish you would have told me that a few hours ago, my legs are shot."

He might not like what was next.

From Muir Beach, we began an arduous climb up to Pantoll Station and Mount Tamalpias. The ascent was brutal, but majestic. The lore of the interconnected network of trails is legendary. Some of the first off-road trail running took place on the nearby historic Dipsea Trail. The sport of mountain biking was born along these trails in the late sixties, when Gary Fisher was suspended from bike racing because his hair was too long. So he took his sport to the hills, and the rest is history.

When we reached Pantoll Station, the first indications of dawn began faintly highlighting the eastern skyline. Topher looked tired. This was natural. Running straight through the night was a new experience to him and going without sleep for twenty-four hours is draining, especially when you layer a fifty-mile training run on top of it.

I had just the solution.

We ran down Mount Tam, banked left on the Dipsea Trail, and followed the path to downtown Mill Valley. We returned to humanity, strategically exiting the trail at precisely the right juncture. Why, you might ask? Because there's a Peet's Coffee in downtown Mill Valley. Peet's Major Dickason's Blend is a staple among endurance athletes during times of extreme fatigue and exhaustion.

Walking into Peet's, I closed my eyes and inhaled, intoxicated by the day's delectable aroma.

While ordering two large cups of the good major's brew, I spotted a familiar friend.

"Should I get some more beans?" I asked Topher.

"Dude, that goes without saying!"

With two freshly brewed cups of piping hot Major D, and a renewed supply of chocolate-covered espresso beans, we exited Peet's with a smile and newfound motivation.

The sun was now hitting the tops of nearby trees. We followed a popular bike-and-jogging path through Sausalito that would eventually lead us to the north side of the Golden Gate Bridge. We were in a residential area now, and although it was still early in the morning, there were plenty of people moving about.

Along with being a central nervous system stimulant, one of the most pronounced pharmacologic effects of caffeine is its inducement of smooth muscle contractions (of which the lower colon is largely composed). Caffeine also has diuretic properties and can increase urine production.

"Karno, I gotta go."

"Here? We're in a family neighborhood."

"I can't hold it."

"Okay, just quickly and discreetly water those hedges over there. I'll watch your back."

"You don't understand. I gotta go big potty."

"What?"

"I gotta go number two. You know, lighten the load."

"Dude, that's problematic."

"You're telling me! I'm about 9.5 on the 10-point Richter scale!"

"All right, all right, calm down. We'll deal."

"That's easy for *you* to say. I gotta go!"

"Do you have any TP?"

"No."

"Can you hold it for half a mile? There's a bathroom up ahead."

"I can't hold it for another ten feet!"

He ran over to the nearest outcropping of bushes and tucked below them. He was directly in front of a school.

"Karno, you need to find me some toilet paper," he yelled from behind the bush.

"On it."

Being Saturday, there was nobody in the school. One of the outside doors was unlocked, so I took the liberty of entering the building. Once inside, I quickly located a men's bathroom, where I spooled a tidy amount of TP around a twig. On my way out the door, I noticed a sampler of carpeting lying on the ground, the type a salesperson might use to display the various varieties and color choices a manufacturer had to offer. I picked it up and took it with me.

I brought the sales sample to Topher and handed it to him over the hedges.

"What's this?" he asked.

"It's all I could find."

"Carpet samples?"

"It's the best I could do."

"I can't use this. It's too abrasive."

"Beggars can't be choosers," I said. "My advice is to use the shag sample. The shorter weaves might be harsh."

Just as he was preparing to start the cleanup, I stopped him and handed over the coil of toilet paper. Needless to say, he was relieved.

After that brief though rather traumatic episode, we resumed forward progress. Passing along the waterfront in Sausalito, we watched the sun gleaming off the bay. The view got even better when we began crossing the Golden Gate Bridge on our way back to San Francisco.

No longer tired and weary, Topher naturally hastened his pace. We began running at six-minute-mile pace, a respectable clip, especially given our past ten hours. Neither of us felt drained. The effects of the bright sunlight on our faces and the jolt of inspiration provided courtesy of Major Dickason did the trick.

When we returned to my house, I took a good look at Topher. He didn't appear haggard. He didn't appear beat up. He didn't appear withered. We had just run fifty-five miles straight through the night, and he looked like one hundred percent pure, unadulterated energy. The kind of energy it would take to tackle the Western States 100-Mile Endurance Run.

▶ Dean and Topher at the start of the Western States 100-Mile Endurance Run

13.0

What's Your Scene?

"It was suddenly so clear: The Terminator would never stop."
—LINDA HAMILTON, AS SARAH CONNOR

HOLLYWOOD HAS MADE its share of running films—some of them good, some of them bad, most of them somewhere in between. There are a few notable exceptions, however. Who can forget the epic struggles of Eric Liddell (Ian Charleson), a determined Christian Scotsman who believed he must succeed as a testament to his undying commitment to God, and Harold Abrahams (Ben Cross), a Jewish Englishman who wanted desperately to prove his place in Cambridge society, in the classic Chariots of Fire?

"I believe God made me for a purpose, but He also made me fast. And when I run I feel His pleasure," says Liddell. Powerful stuff.

People sometimes ask me what my favorite running clips have been, knowing that a flashback to a funny or upbeat scene can provide a bolt of invigoration, especially during longer runs.

In *Forrest Gump* there are endearing scenes: "I just felt like running." Which meant back and forth across the country several times.

And in another classic scene, a man in the bumper sticker business runs after Forrest and solicits his help. Since Forrest has been such an inspiration to so many people, the man thinks he might be able to come up with an inspiring slogan and move some bumper stickers. As the two men are running along, the bumper sticker man notices that Forrest has just run through a big pile of, well, shit.

"Whoa," the man says. "You just stepped in a big pile of dog shit."

Forrest replies, "It happens."

"What? Shit?" asks the bumper sticker man.

"Sometimes," says Forrest, cool as ever.

The brilliance of *Forrest Gump* is that interwoven between these scenes of quirky providence are evocative and more meaningful moments: "I don't know if we each have a destiny, or if we're all just floatin' around accidental-like on a breeze. But I, I think maybe it's both."

But perhaps my favorite movie scene of all time has nothing to do with the act of running per se (though I would argue the underlying theme relates directly to running).

It's from a much-loved, though relatively obscure, movie called *Never Cry Wolf*. The film was a small-scale production that never received much hype or media attention. It's a great picture nonetheless, and one of the opening scenes is an absolute classic. A young urban biologist named Tyler (played by Charles Martin Smith) is being flown into the Arctic outback by a bush pilot named Rosie (played by Brian Dennehy). Tyler is going there to study the dwindling native caribou population.

During Rosie's flight across the vast Arctic wilderness in his antiquated airplane, his engine begins to sputter and choke, then completely stalls out. He starts cursing at the plane and banging on the controls. Meanwhile, Tyler is becoming concerned, and justifiably so. Rosie tells Tyler to reach under his seat and hand him a wrench out of a rusting tool chest. When Tyler finally locates the tool and hands it to him, Rosie starts climbing out the airplane window to get to the engine.

Tyler starts freaking out. He frantically asks, "What's wrong? What's wrong?"

Rosie turns back to him. "What's wrong?" he asks. "What's wrong, Tyler? I'll tell you what's wrong," as he edges farther out the plane's window. "Boredom, Tyler, that's what's wrong. Boredom."

Tyler is now staring at him in disbelief. Rosie turns back one last time. "And do you know what the cure for boredom is, Tyler? Adventure!" He thrusts the wrench into the air, then proceeds to climb entirely out the plane's window.

I thought of that scene often when, sitting listlessly in my office cubicle, someone asked, "What's wrong?"

• • • •

Of all the running scenes I've watched, though, my top pick would have to be from *Terminator 2: Judgment Day*. Put James Cameron behind the camera and a not-yet-political Arnold Schwarzenegger in front of it, and you've got one of the greatest action flicks ever.

The main character in this scene is not Arnold, however, but the next-generation Terminator (Robert Patrick), who's been summoned to earth to terminate the original Terminator. In this segment, the new Terminator has morphed into a traffic cop. He identifies his target in a passing car, the young John Connor, and begins pursuit on foot, eventually building up to an impressive run. Arnold pops out of the car's window holding a sawed-off shotgun and unloads on the T-1000. The nuevo Terminator takes the shotgun hit, stumbles slightly, and then resumes chase.

Arnold then whips out a rocket launcher and nails the T-1000 squarely in the melon, splitting his head in two. This knocks him down. Lying on the ground, his head in two pieces, he begins to regroup. Slowly, he crawls back to his feet, stands up, and keeps running.

A flurry of high-powered explosives is then unleashed upon him by Arnold and John's mom, Sarah, blowing the pursuant to absolute smithereens. His body is shattered into a million tiny pieces. Arnold, John, and Sarah drive off into the distance, thinking that he's been completely annihilated. Gradually, Terminator 2.0 begins to reconstitute. Bit by bit, he pulls himself back together. He shakes off the temporary setback and rises to his feet, determined to never stop.

I've seen a few friends come back from the dead during long races, and I always chuckle and think of that scene.

• • • •

Great running movie moments would not be complete without paying homage to the late Steve Prefontaine. In the movie *Without*

Limits, he leaves us with a timeless piece of wisdom stated in a way that only Pre could have put it: "Giving anything less than your best is to sacrifice the gift."

Let's hope that one day Hollywood gets it right and produces another legit running flick. Until then, long live Pre! (And the Terminator!)

14.0

Living with an Athlete

"Love will tear us apart."
—JOY DIVISION

ENDURANCE SPORTS WILL either strengthen a relationship or destroy it. There's no middle ground. I have witnessed relationships and families grow stronger when one partner, or even one sibling, takes up running, cycling, or triathlon. On the flip side, I have seen relationships torn apart.

Endurance sports are, by nature, polarizing. They can (some might say they *must*) be all-consuming. Participants tend to be deeply devoted and fanatical (again, some might say they *must* be deeply devoted and fanatical to succeed). These are simply the qualities needed to excel in such sports.

Is this a bad thing? Not necessarily. These same personality traits can lead to great devotion and dedication to a relationship and to a family. That is the bright side. The dark side is that such individuals can easily appear obsessive and self-absorbed (and many may actually be both of these).

Over the years, I've had plenty of people ask about my relationship with my wife, Julie, and my family. On the surface, we seem to have a fairly harmonious coexistence. But perhaps that's just my own egocentric viewpoint. Many people have asked for Julie's take on the matter.

Instead of putting words in her mouth, I thought it would be interesting to let her answer the question of what it's like living with an athlete herself. So, my love, run with it . . .

Meet the Dean Karnazes I Know
By Julie Karnazes

When someone asks me what life is like living with the "Ultramarathon Man," I usually take just a moment to ponder how best to answer this question. Having known Dean for the past thirty-one years, we've spent most of our lives together. Since the beginning of our relationship back in high school, I've watched a driven, intelligent, and devoted boy grow up into one incredible man. Let me tell you a little bit about the Dean Karnazes I know.

ON PREPARING FOR A RACE: Dean is an organized and methodical person (thank goodness!). Here's an example of the systematic approach he used to prepare for one of his ultramarathon races: After work one foggy San Francisco summer eve, I entered our living room to find every inch of available floor space occupied with massive piles of gear, food, clothing, and special equipment. The walls were adorned with maps held in place by blue painter's tape.

Written in big, bold black ink at the top of each map was a time and a mile marker. As I quietly stood there watching, Dean began strategically shuffling the masses of special clothing, water bottles, headlamps, GU packets, and shoes beneath each of the handmade signs.

Dean finally noticed me watching him and jumped up to give me a hug. With a twinkle in his eye, he explained his system. "Simple," he said, "you just place the stuff you need according to your anticipated pace over a twenty-four-hour period." He spoke about running for twenty-four straight hours the way others might talk about taking the dog for a walk around the park.

Our living room looked more like a strategic command center readying the troops for battle than a place to have a relaxing dinner. Oh well, so much for unwinding in my favorite room after a long day at the office. I offered to help, but he insisted that I just sit back and relax. Then he ordered us Thai food from my favorite restaurant down the street. I told him that he had my full support to race frequently and often!

ON SLEEP: Someone once asked me about the amount of sleep Dean gets each night. My face contorted. "Sleep? My husband does not sleep."

If I calculated all the restless nights we've been together, I figure Ultramarathon Man owes me about fifteen years of sleep. Dean seems to function perfectly well on four hours per night. I, on the other hand, require a traditional eight (sometimes ten on the weekends is nice!).

Imagine, if you will, being perpetually awakened night after restless night because your loving partner keeps tossing and turning. After weeks of repeated nighttime rousing, I'm left in a state of mental fuzziness. Perhaps he can't sleep because he's contemplating an upcoming race, or perhaps it's writer's block, or perhaps he's working on composing a keynote speech; whatever the cause of his restlessness, I'm sometimes rendered incapacitated by it.

The solution I've found is to have the man go running. This remedy occurred naturally one morning after yet another sleepless night. I remember him informing me that he'd intentionally stayed awake all night to finish a project that he'd been working on. Great, I laughed. Great! Instead of sleeping just four hours a night he was going to give up sleep altogether.

Then Dean divulged his sleepless epiphany. "Do not try to override your body's natural rhythm," he told me. "Next time, I think I'll just run all night."

"Sure," I said, "go with the flow." I encouraged him, but I was actually selfishly thinking this might be a mechanism for me to get some sleep!

A couple nights later, on Friday, I heard him rustling around downstairs going through his running gear after reading to the kids in bed. He asked me if I'd like to spend the weekend in Calistoga, a bucolic little town some seventy miles from our house in

San Francisco. He said he was going to run up there. Our family loves Calistoga, so of course I agreed—thinking of one thing only: a full night's sleep!

With the kids tucked away quietly, he gave me a peck on the cheek and headed out the door. I, on the other hand, hunkered down for a night of uninterrupted slumber. As much as I missed him, it was luxurious not having a wild animal tossing around all night next to me.

When we awoke on Saturday morning, I loaded the kids in the car and headed off to Calistoga. Dean arrived about the same time we did. The only difference: He'd traveled on foot. We rendezvoused at our favorite breakfast nook and enjoyed a leisurely morning meal. Then we spent a relaxing weekend swimming and playing around Calistoga and the Napa Valley.

We all enjoyed the experience so much that Dean incorporated the routine into his normal training program. It was great for everybody. We got to travel to different places on the weekends and explore the best of the Bay Area. The kids got to experience new things, Dean got to run, and I got to sleep!

ON LIVING WITH SOMEONE FAMOUS: What's it like living with someone who's famous? I'm not exactly sure. The Dean I live with takes out the trash, shops at the grocery store, and attends parent-teacher conferences, activities not typically associated with someone famous. Sometimes I forget *Time* magazine designated him as one of the "Top 100 Most Influential People in the World," one behind George Clooney and ahead of Oprah.

Then I'm reminded of his notoriety when there's a "Dean

sighting." The first thing I see people do is whisper to each other. "That's him," they say. "Did you see him?" They motion excitedly. "That's the Ultramarathon Man!" "Look, it's Team Dean!" "There goes Karno!"

It feels funny to hear them referring to my husband in the third person. They know him as an author, an accomplished runner, and a passionate advocate for healthy, active living. To his fans, he's famous. To me, Dean is just a boy I fell in love with. He's the guy who makes me homemade soup when I'm sick, the guy who meticulously cleans our windows because that's the way I like it, and the guy who cares deeply for our children. I've accepted the fact that he's become "famous," but he's never really changed from the boy I once knew.

Dean always jokes with me. "You know, he says, "behind every successful man is a very surprised woman." But I think *he's* more surprised by his success than I am. To be honest, I don't think he views himself as "successful" at all. He's got awards, plaques, trophies, medals, and governmental honor certificates sitting in boxes in our garage. I don't think any of this stuff means anything to him. He remains one of the most humble and least pretentious people I know.

Some people might imagine that fame has brought fortune with it. Sure, Dean has realized some prosperity, and rightfully so. He's changed countless lives for the better. Still, he remains one of the least material people I've ever met. "Things" simply don't matter to him. He values people, experiences, learning, exploration. He just doesn't seem to care about material possessions. Influencing someone to change their life for the better brings him more joy than a million dollars ever could.

That's the famous Dean Karnazes I know.

ON RUNNING: Sometimes during my husband's events I'm asked, "Are *you* a runner?"

I always stammer and shuffle my feet. I'd like to answer, "Yes, I am." But instead, I answer by explaining that I am not a runner.

That's not to say that I *haven't* run. In high school, I used to run four miles on the beach nearly every afternoon. I still vividly remember the sound of the sand crunching under my shoes and feeling the salt on my cheeks afterward. I quite enjoyed it. So, yes, I *have* run, but I am no longer "a runner."

Sometimes I do picture the two of us running at sunset as the light in the sky turns a romantic faint purple-blue. Then I'd be able to answer the inquisitor's question with, "Yes, I am a runner," and they would smile and think to themselves, *I knew it . . . I knew it! They run together!*

The reason I feel uncomfortable answering this question is because sometimes people look so disappointed when they learn that I am not a runner. I've often thought about running again, not so much to avoid these disappointed looks, but because in reflecting back to high school, I liked running. Well, what do you know, Ultramarathon Man's magic might just be working on me, too.

ON THE "REAL STORY": Okay, maybe I've painted a picture of Dean that's all roses. Clearly, I have the utmost admiration and respect for him, but that's not to say he's perfect.

The man can be bullheaded, annoyingly so at times. He's principled almost to a fault. But he's never afraid to admit he's wrong. He's open-minded and always willing to listen to opposing viewpoints and perspectives. He's amazingly open to criticism, almost welcomes it. I think he's mostly interested in being a better person and in doing what's right rather than satisfying his ego.

Other weaknesses: He can be a pushover, especially with the kids. I know he feels guilty sometimes about the amount of time he spends away. So he spoils them rotten. He spoils me, too.

On that topic, let me give all you nonrunning partners out there a bit of insider's advice: The best time to ask for something is during the postrace afterglow. Your runner will likely be giddy with endorphins and slightly weakened from the run. They're highly vulnerable during this small window of opportunity.

Here are some of my recent successes after a good, long run by Dean:

"Darling, about that remodeling job we've been discussing . . . " Enough said. Approved!

"Honey, the mileage on our car is creeping up and I really like the new . . . " Done!

"Sweetie, the newspapers have been advertising these great vacation deals to . . . " Booked!

His faults are remarkably few, so I've got to capitalize on every one of them!

In closing, reporters are always asking me, "Why does your husband run? Is he running from something? To something? Which one is it?"

It's neither, I've come to realize. Dean runs for one reason, and one reason only: because he loves to run.

15.0

First Is Best

By Topher Gaylord

"Run like hell and get the agony over with."
—Clarence DeMar

WHEN THE IMPOSSIBLE suddenly becomes possible, the mind expands and the world grows. My first Western States 100-Mile Endurance Run was one of those mind-expanding moments in time that I will remember forever.

I first met Dean Karnazes as a teenager in the early eighties while windsurfing the shark-infested waters off the California coast. We shared a kindred spirit of pushing the edges of our potential in life, and we found those edges in sport. Dean and I frequently shared adventures and stories after long days of windsurfing. I remember one of those days in the early nineties when he announced to me that he intended to run a hundred-mile race through the rugged mountains of California. At first, I simply did not believe him. There was no way a human being could run one hundred miles without dying. It simply wasn't possible.

When he promised me that it was possible, my questions were incessant: How long does it take? What do you eat? How do you go to the bathroom? What do you drink? How many people in the world attempt this? Are you joking? No way!

But there was a way. It took me nearly a decade to believe it and develop an appetite to actually want to try it. Dean was the catalyst that sparked my curiosity and encouraged me to test the edges of my own potential in running. When I did, my life was forever changed.

Here's how my first Western States 100 unfolded.

It started with a very restless night's sleep. I finally awoke to a rooster alarm, compliments of Karno. We were up at 3:00 A.M., and I began the meticulous process and ritual of preparing for the epic journey ahead. Shorts, shirt, sunscreen, lubrication in key chafing zones, nipple Band-Aids, race number, water bottles, food, socks, and shoes. Tying my laces just right, not too tight, not too loose. I opened the window of my room and the cold Sierra Mountain air poured in, crisp, fresh, and energizing.

Kimmy, who was my girlfriend at the time, had been an amazing source of strategy, support, encouragement, and energy throughout my preparation for this momentous undertaking. She was my crew chief and would be pacing me along the latter section of the race late in the night. I felt a commitment to give this run everything I had to not only achieve my goal, but to honor all the sacrifices she had made for me.

Kim and I had discussed my eating strategy in detail, and she had found mini ice chests to use as drop bags out on the course. The race organizers place drop bags at aid stations, most of which are inaccessible to the crews, for the runners to access during the event.

This would be a unique year at Western States. Due to heavy spring snow conditions, the course was rerouted and I would not see my crew for the first fifty-five miles. Usually you can see them at mile thirty. However, Kim is very thorough. She placed written instructions in each drop bag to remind me of the "strategy." A good crew and pacers are a massive source of energy and I had the best, with Kim leading my crew of family and close friends.

Dean and I had talked a lot about strategy; he had been a great coach and training partner over the ten months leading up to the race. He emphasized that it is always better to leave some energy for the later miles and finish strong. We talked a lot about the twenty-four-hour silver buckle—one of the most coveted prizes in hundred-mile endurance running. Many runners become fixated on finishing in under twenty-four hours in an effort to win this coveted symbol of running endurance. "Bucklemania," it's been called. They make massive pacing errors or simply run beyond their capabilities and not only do they miss the twenty-four-hour buckle, but many fail to finish. I committed to two simple goals that I would repeat to myself before the race and during the race: 1) Don't stop until you get to the finish line. 2) Don't worry about how long it takes; run within yourself.

The Western States 100-Mile Endurance Run is a contest of extremes. My first year, in particular, was over the top. It had been an enormous winter with record snowfall and a very cool spring.

On race day—which is always held on the last weekend of June—the course was covered in over six feet of snow from Squaw Valley to Duncan Canyon, mile twenty-four. There was so much snow on the course, we would be running nearly a marathon in the snow. I loved the snow and grew up ski racing, but the thought of running twenty-four miles in it seemed impossible. In fact, due to the snow the course was diverted and rerouted from mile twenty-four to mile forty, where it rejoined the normal Western States course.

To add to the complexity, the high temperature in the notorious "canyons" section was forecasted to be 105 degrees. Fire and ice. Knowing these types of conditions were likely, I spent the months and weeks prior to race day reinforcing the saying: "Whatever the conditions are on race day, I will embrace and love them."

Dean, Jim Vernon, and I made our final prerace preparations at the house we were sharing. We then made our way over to the start of the race. I felt like a boxer entering an arena, small steps, nervous energy, excitement. It was 4:30 A.M., and lights illuminated the first five hundred yards of the course that goes straight up the guts of the Squaw Valley Ski Resort. We were starting at the base of the ski lifts, elevation 6,200 feet. Crew members and runners called out each other's names. Cameras flashed, videographers filmed, the *Rocky* theme played in the background, and massive energy coursed through my veins. It was simply electrifying! Every nerve fiber in my body was twitching with the anticipation of taking on a challenge so big, so far beyond my comprehension, so immense. Others appeared to have this buzz going, too. Some were trying to internally harness the energy, stay calm, and save every drop for the run itself; others simply couldn't contain themselves and belted out wild noises, snorts, yodels, hoots, fist pumps, high fives, and chest bumps. A few seconds before the start, Dean and I embraced in a hug and shared some brief words of encouragement. I told him I wasn't stopping until I got to Auburn! He wished me the best of luck.

The gun went off at 5:00 A.M. and four hundred runners embarked on a journey of a lifetime to run one hundred miles in a single day. Some, like me, were running this distance for the first time; others had run the distance more than fifty times, but none was guaranteed to finish. We took off running straight up the steepest ski run of the mountain, a 2,600-foot climb straight to the summit. From there, it's ninety-six miles across the Sierra Nevada mountains to Auburn, California.

I sprinted from the start on fresh legs. I started pounding the first climb. Within minutes I felt as if I had seared my lungs from the fast initial effort. My mouth felt as if it were stuffed with cotton balls and my breathing became labored. I backed it down, drank some water, and tried to develop a rhythm of my own. As we climbed out of Squaw Valley, the alpenglow across the mountains and the sun to the east filled the day with vivid color. As we crested the escarpment, the high point of the course, the sun's first rays hit the highest peaks, firing light across the mountains.

The profound immensity of the day was overwhelmingly emotional, and my eyes welled up with tears of joy. I was now on this journey into the unknown, surrounded by nature and others who were also taking on this immense challenge, all connected by a common goal: reaching Auburn.

As we made our way across the Sierra high country, there was snow as far as the eye could see. The going was slow to Lyons Ridge, an early aid station at eleven miles. The course was tricky here, a bit of a side hill, and the snow was sun-cupped. Many runners were breaking through the snow and "post holing" to their thighs in soft spots around tree wells. Others were slipping and sliding, some falling and sliding off the course down the hill, self-arresting with their water bottles and fingertips. Falling on ice and snow in the summer is like falling on a cheese grater, and many runners were falling and getting eaten up by the "snow grater," blood oozing from their knees, elbows, and other body parts. I resorted to a unique running technique of jumping from sun-cup ridge to sun-cup ridge. It required massive concentration, balance, and a bizarre gait. Approaching Lyons Ridge, I reached down for an energy gel, and in that flash of distraction I too found myself flat on my face. Damage report: one oozing bloody knee. The pain seemed to be just a burning slice in my knee, so I continued on, hoping it would not become a major problem later in the run.

Just past Lyons Ridge, I felt a blister developing in my foot from this sun-cup running style. I was just twelve miles into the run. My mind raced: How could I possibly manage a blister for another eighty-eight miles?

I kept myself focused. The snow running continued for the first twenty-four miles into Duncan Canyon. As I approached the first major aid station in the race, my pace quickened as I was being cheered on by volunteers. I used the aid station to change out of my wet shoes and socks, took my planned food from the drop bag that Kim had prepared, and thanked the volunteers for their support. I was feeling good and happy that I had safely navigated the most challenging section of the course.

Soon after departing the aid station, I encountered my first major low. The sun beat down on my head, I was hot, the food I ate was not sitting well, and my legs felt heavy. Wow, things can change rapidly, I thought to myself. At Western States they say, "If you feel good, just wait a minute."

Western States is a unique race with respect to camaraderie. Yes, the front of the course is a competitive race, with all the accompanying tactics, but every runner in a hundred-mile race suffers immensely and faces various forms of self-doubt. This is true whether you are the first-place finisher or the last. This kindred spirit and shared experience creates a feeling of support during this colossal test of endurance. So, when one runner is suffering, a fellow runner might offer up some words of encouragement, hope, or suggestions. This type of support is what makes ultra running such a unique sport and creates deep bonds within the greater ultra running community.

In my deep low, another runner came up beside me and provided me with encouragement and suggestions to ease my nausea. His support lifted me and helped my mind remain committed to the task at hand.

As I arrived at Dusty Corners, I was able to muscle down some watermelon and boiled potatoes dipped in salt. I washed it all down with a Snickers and took off running.

Last Chance aid station, at mile forty-three, comes at a brutal time in the Western States course. You have been running long enough to feel the effects of deep fatigue in your body, it is very hot, the tough "canyons" section of the run is still ahead of you, and you have to deal mentally with the thought of running fifty-seven more miles when you're already quite destroyed.

The Last Chance aid station volunteers greeted the runners with enthusiasm, but were focused on keeping us moving. Stopping for too long at any aid station can prove disastrous, as you may never start again. They gave me my drop bag of sandwiches, nuts, energy drinks, and additional provisions. The volunteer looked inside and said, "Wow, what can I get for you?" Nothing looked good; I was white in the face, my head was spinning, and the thought of eating anything made me sick. I looked at the volunteer and said, "Please close the icebox, it is making me sick." They offered me soup and I slurped some down; it was the only calories I could consume. I'd fallen off my eating plan, but I was still moving forward.

At mile forty-five, you cross a bridge at the bottom of a deep canyon and start the steepest climb of the course up to the Devils Thumb aid station, a brutal 1,800-foot ascent. (For comparison, the infamous "Heartbreak Hill" at the Boston Marathon rises just 270 feet.) I looked down at my watch. It read 104 degrees. As I ran across the bridge and took my first step up this monster climb, the taste of nickels filled my mouth. I was on the verge of vomiting, and I had taken just one step up this climb; tens of thousands still remained. And this was only the first of several canyons to contend with along the course.

It was a desperate moment. I stopped, bent over, head throbbing, heat engulfing me. I couldn't move. I sat down on a rock to try and regroup. My race plan was in complete disarray; I hadn't eaten more than some watermelon, a couple slurps of soup, and one small bottle of water since Duncan Canyon nearly twenty miles ago.

After a few minutes, I reminded myself of my mission: "Don't stop until you get to Auburn." And I thought of my crew that was waiting anxiously for me all day at mile fifty-five. I decided that I must make it to the top of this climb, to the next aid station. I began moving. Runners came by with words of encouragement, but I didn't hear them; my ears were ringing, I was blurry-eyed, and I was weaving from side to side. The nausea was overwhelming, and I was resigned to the fact that I might not make it to the finish at Western States.

You learn to be successful in ultra running, or you never finish. As in life, you must be able to adapt your mind when your run is not going as planned. This was one of those moments. I had my eating, drinking, and pacing plans all mapped out at the start of the race. Split times were written down neatly in each of my drop bags to remind me where I was and how I was doing against my goal. All elements of my plan were now out the window. I couldn't eat or drink, and I had fallen behind my expected pace, which created a sense of urgency and desperation. It's at moments like these that you need to dig deep, stay focused, and remind yourself to concentrate on the small goals, not letting the enormity of the miles still ahead consume your mind with negative thoughts. Just focus on what you can control right now, and that was the simple task of putting one foot in front of the other.

After painfully slow progress, I finally made it to the top of the Devils Thumb aid station. They tell you at the prerace briefing to "beware of the chair," as runners frequently get here, sit in the chairs at the aid station, and never get up. I flopped into a chair, ghost white, head between my hands, panting like a dog. A volunteer was offering me crackers, soup, Coca-Cola, fruit. I couldn't eat any of it. After several minutes in the chair, I was able to sip some soda and slurp a bit of soup. Someone applied some cold ice directly to my head, and I started to come back to life. The volunteers stood me up, asked some questions, got the right answers, and sent me on my way.

As I started down a long section of trail that plunged 2,500 feet into El Dorado Canyon, I began to get a nice cadence going. Fantastic, I thought, I'm coming back. This thought quickly departed as I crossed the bridge at the bottom of the canyon and began the long climb up to Michigan Bluff. Nausea returned with a vengeance, and I reined in my goals, simply setting my sights on making it to the next aid station.

I approached the Michigan Bluff aid station, mentally lifted at the thought of seeing my support crew. There is an intimate bond between a hundred-mile runner and his crew. Crews are not merely spectators offering encouragement; they can be a key contributor to any ultra runner's success. They can lift even the most exhausted runner's spirits, providing nourishment for the soul at a time when many are too nauseated to take in any literal nourishment.

Arriving at Michigan Bluff, I was out of energy, queasy, completely fatigued, and totally overheated. Kim and my crew went to work on me immediately, changing my shoes, socks, and shirt, applying ice to my head, feeding me soup and Coca-Cola—along with a healthy load of motivating words. Their energy revived me; I was exhausted physically, but I was renewed mentally. I needed it. At Western States it is said that you run the first fifty miles with your legs, and the next fifty miles with your mind. I was embarking deep into unknown territory, mentally and physically. I had never run more than fifty miles before. I had no idea of whether my body could truly handle a hundred miles, but I was resolved to try.

I thought about Dean and Jim a lot during the run. I wondered how they were doing. Information was scarce along the course. The folks at the aid stations had their hands full with trying to tend to the immediate needs of the incoming runners, many of whom were in dire straits and needed prompt assistance. The aid station personnel weren't always able to keep track of which runners had come and gone. I hadn't seen either Dean or Jim lying flat on the trailside, so I presumed they were surviving.

The next stop was at Foresthill, mile sixty-two, and the point in the race where you can have a pacer join you. My oldest brother, Terry, was scheduled to run the section of trail with me from mile sixty-two to seventy-eight, terminating at the Rucky Chucky river crossing.

As we left Foresthill, I had been running for fourteen hours, and the sun was now low in the sky. Finally, the slightly cooler air began to breathe life back into my legs, and my running with Terry felt at times effortless. I was still unable to eat any food, still powered completely by soup broth and Coca-Cola.

As the evening turned to night, we switched on our lights and continued down the trail. On the way down to the river we came across a runner who was lying in the middle of the trail, sound asleep with his pacer standing over him. I thought we were witnessing a major emergency. Terry and I immediately stopped and asked if the runner was okay; his pacer confirmed to us that he was just taking a "little rest." He looked dead, but we were assured he was only sleeping. So we continued down the trail toward the river.

Crossing the middle fork of the American River at the Rucky Chucky rapid, the snow runoff was so intense and the currents so strong that they ferried the runners across the river in rubber boats tethered to a safety line. The crossing was still hairy. Kim was on the other side of the river. She had every type of food for me, but I simply couldn't eat; my nausea continued, and soup and cola were my only remedies.

Kim and Terry traded pacing duties at mile eighty. It was now very dark. As Kim and I set out on the trail together, we stepped over more carnage. Runners lay sound asleep on the ground, others stood on the side of the trail vomiting, and some lay out on stretchers at aid stations with IVs in their arms from exhaustion.

Laura Vaughn, an exceptional ultra runner, told me prior to the race, "Topher, using energy in a hundred-mile run is like money in the bank. You only have a certain amount of it, and you have to make it last to the end. If you run too hard too early, you can find yourself later in the race without enough energy to make it to the finish. You can't get it back, no deposits during the race, so spend your energy wisely."

Many of these destroyed runners had spent too much of their energy early in the day, and they had nothing left in the bank. I, too, was on the brink, finding myself falling asleep on the trail as we made our way along looking for the next glow stick that marked the path. I tried shaking my head back and forth, tried as hard as I could to will the fatigue and sleep deprivation from my body, but nothing cleared the mounting drowsiness.

Kim provided me the right words of encouragement at the right times, and her energy was helping lift my spirits and my pace. We had a strong section together coming into the Highway 49 aid station, mile ninety-four, just on the cusp of the twenty-four-hour pace. When running a marathon, they talk about "hitting the wall"; when running a hundred miles, you hit multiple walls. The walls get thicker the farther you progress, and breaking through them gets more difficult.

At the Highway 49 aid station, Kim traded places with Todd Katz—a work colleague—who would be my final pacer. We took off quickly in an effort to go for the twenty-four-hour buckle. It was going to be close. With just six miles left to run, I could now begin to "taste the finish," though only mildly. Then, a mere three minutes out of the aid station, I hit a brutal wall. This one was horrendous. Again I was weaving back and forth on the trail, dead tired, stumbling, and semicoherent. I had gotten ahead of myself with Kim, running strong, and now I felt like I had nothing left. Had I spent all my money? Runners began passing me, all going for that elusive sub-twenty-four-hour time. Just three minutes earlier I, too, wanted to go for it; now my principal concern was whether I'd be able to finish at all. Jim Vernon passed me at this point and provided some encouraging words that injected me with a shot of energy. I was grateful for his friendship in that moment of deep darkness.

We crested yet another climb and began the final four-mile stretch. If there were any funds left in the bank, now would be the time to make that final withdrawal. I was dying. The Western States finish has a stinger in the tail; there is an absolutely killer climb the final two miles of the course.

But with just two miles left to go, the final check cleared and the money was deposited for spending. So I spent! For the first time in over twenty-three hours, I felt I could make it.

We crested the top of the final climb, ran down into Auburn, and entered the famous Auburn High School Stadium for the final loop on the track where the finish line was erected. My entire crew joined me, and we ran the final four hundred yards together to the finish. Tears filled my eyes from the fatigue and joy of accomplishing the impossible! I crossed the finish line in twenty-three hours and forty-two minutes. I had finished my first Western States 100-Mile Endurance Run and was a proud winner of the coveted silver buckle award.

As I crossed the finish line, my entire body began to seize up. I was physically annihilated. Every bone and muscle was burning with pain, but my mind was firing with life, joy, energy, and emotion.

One hundred miles, 17,000 feet of climbing, 22,000 feet of descending, rocks, roots, snow, sweltering heat, stream crossings, dust, highs, lows, despair, desperation, joy, and elation.

I had lived a lifetime in a single day. Sharing the moment with my crew of family and close friends moved me. It was a team effort and we had been one of the more fortunate; a third of the racers never finished at all, let alone earn a silver buckle for a sub-twenty-four-hour finish.

Jim, too, cracked twenty-four hours, finishing right before I did. Karno had finished long ago, gotten a night's sleep, and come back to the finish line to congratulate Jim and me. I'll never forget the proud smile on his face, like a father watching his son take his first steps. We embraced and I thanked him for all his support and encouragement.

We all went to breakfast, where Julie and Kimmy took turns fork-feeding me; I was simply too exhausted to lift my arm. Would

I ever attempt anything like this again? It was a transformational experience to be sure. I learned plenty about myself, maybe more than I had known in my lifetime up to then.

At that moment, though, I wasn't thinking about the future. I wasn't even certain I'd ever be able to walk again. All I was thinking about right now was a warm bed and a cold glass of anything other than Coca-Cola.

► Crossing the Atacama Desert salt flats

16.0

4 Deserts and Some Badwater

"The bold don't live forever but the timid don't live at all."

—MARCO POLO

THERE ARE PLACES in the Atacama Desert that have never recorded rain. Ever.

Nothing is alive here. The environment is so mercilessly parched that not even the most resilient of weeds can survive. Exposed crimson outcroppings of bedrock and stone mar the harsh, naked surface, which resembles that of Mars, only more barren. What better place to stage a footrace?

The 4 Deserts races take place in some of the most remote and inhospitable places on earth, Atacama being one such location. These multiday, self-supported events require competitors to carry everything they need to survive while crossing 250 kilometers (155 miles) of the most savage wilderness imaginable (the exception being a daily allotment of water). Why ration water? I guess the race organizers wanted to make it as authentic as possible. This is a race across the desert, after all.

When the founder of the 4 Deserts race series, Mary Gadams, initially contacted me, I was intrigued. The Atacama Crossing race looked intense, but I love a challenge. I told her it might be something I'd like to try.

"I don't just mean the Atacama Crossing," she explained, "I mean the entire 4 Deserts race series."

Now I was a little more than intrigued; I was petrified. The other events consisted of races across the Gobi Desert, the Sahara Desert, and the largest desert on earth, Antarctica. (Many people don't realize Antarctica is a desert. It is. It's just a cold desert. A desert is defined as any region that receives less than twenty-five centimeters—ten inches—of annual rainfall. Antarctica averages less than ten centimeters.) No one had ever completed all four races in the same calendar year.

When someone issues a blanket challenge like this, the brazen accept sight unseen. I told her I'd have to get back to her. There were a few minor details I wanted to explore. Like, had anyone died before?

In doing some research, I noticed that the 4 Deserts organization was headquartered overseas. While I'm no legal eagle, I do know that other countries tend to have more relaxed liability laws than the United States. (Imagine that; in other places you have to actually take responsibility for your own actions.) Hmm, I thought, this is the real deal. Cool. Real risk. I like that.

Plus, the format seemed to suit my strengths perfectly. I've never been known as the most svelte, quickest guy in town. Seeing how fast I could go interested me less than seeing how *far* I could go. When it came to overall endurance and pound-for-pound strength, I could hold my own with the best of them. A grueling multiday event that required carrying a heavy backpack through difficult terrain in extreme weather conditions seemed ideal for my tastes.

Turns out I wasn't the only one contemplating the challenge of attempting all four desert races in the same year. Mary had made the offer public, and three others had enrolled. Two were Europeans, the other South African. All of them hard-core. This was good. Now I was over the edge. I called Mary back and told her I wanted in. Once that call was made, there was no turning back. Like Robert Altman said: "To play it safe is not to play." Let the adventure commence!

• • • •

Just getting to the Atacama Desert in Chile is an endurance event in its own right. I left San Francisco raring to go. Multiple plane flights, airport transfers, shuttles, and bus rides later, I arrived in the remote desert outpost of San Pedro de Atacama with a little less gusto. The sun had just set on my second day of travel.

The one thing that immediately struck me about the Atacama Desert is how cold it got at night. Temperatures during the day peak above a hundred degrees Fahrenheit, but at night it can dip below freezing. I hadn't brought warm enough clothing, but there was not much I could do about it now.

I met the other racers at the mandatory equipment check-in the next morning. Participants are required to carry certain items with them at all times while ambling across the desert for six days (a toothbrush not being one of them). The list includes things like a sleeping bag—but not an accompanying pad—a safety knife, a jacket, night-lights, and at least two thousand calories of food per day. The trick is to be as thrifty as possible ("Light is right") but not overly so ("Go light, freeze at night").

Nobody was more dialed-in than Rob James. A seasoned adventure racer and former British Special Forces member, Rob was a master of efficiency. His pack weighed ten pounds less than mine at check-in.

At the gathering, I also met the other racers vying to be the first to complete all 4 Deserts races in a single calendar year: Jimmy Olsen, Ken "Tintin" Johansson, and Paul Liebenberg. Although there was plenty of camaraderie and well wishes, I think we were sizing each other up a bit, too.

Jimmy was the youngest and lived in Europe, though he traveled extensively to compete. He was lean and fast. The year prior, he had competed in one of the 4 Deserts events, the Sahara Race, and won it convincingly. The kid definitely looked like a contender.

So did Tintin, though in a different sort of way. A professional endurance athlete, he was built more sturdily and low to the ground. A survivalist, Tintin was known as someone who could deal with untold pain and suffering and still keep going. His racing tactics were reminiscent of the Buddha's quote: "Endurance is one of the most difficult disciplines, but it is to the one who endures that the final victory comes."

Paul was a South African living in Australia. Charismatic and bright, he was both an Ironman and a physician. Paul was very likeable—always quick with a joke and incredibly witty—and he kept the group around him entertained. And there was usually a group around him, drawn to his energy and easygoing charm. He was tall, tan, and bright-eyed, with a perpetual look of boyish mischief on his face.

I'm not sure what the others thought of me. I didn't say a whole lot. I quietly watched the racers go through their routines, analyzing the ways they packed their gear, whittled weight from their mandatory equipment, and readied their shoes and clothing for the upcoming challenge. I wanted to learn as much as possible—less in the hope of becoming a more fierce competitor than merely wanting to maximize the odds of my survival.

• • • •

DAY ONE We'd been transported to a desolate desert location where each runner was assigned to a group tent. Your tentmates would either become your best friends over the next six nights, or your worst enemies. My compatriots seemed like a decent group (i.e., they were all relatively small so they didn't occupy too much of the cramped interior real estate, and none of them snored too loudly). Still, I couldn't sleep a wink that first night.

The one element I'd failed to condition for in my training and preparation was altitude. Yes, altitude. You typically think of a desert as being at sea level—or below, as in the case of Death Valley—but much of Atacama is high desert. All night long I tossed and turned, attempting to get comfortable on the cold, rocky desert floor. When the first rays of sunlight began piercing the crisp morning stillness, I gave up trying. There would be no sleep on this first night in the desert.

When the starting gun went off, the racers blazed out at a

blistering clip, which concerned me. Should I chase the leaders or settle back into a more comfortable pace? With the jet lag, sleep deprivation, lack of acclimatization, and my heavy pack, I decided to hold back. I didn't have much control over the matter, actually.

By the midway point of the first stage of racing, however, there was already heavy carnage along the course. People were hurting big time. My need-imposed strategy of going out slowly was paying off. I began passing runner after runner who struggled along the difficult course. Eventually I passed the entire field and survived Stage 1 of the Atacama Crossing in first place. The Yellow Jersey, presented to the overall leader to wear during each of the six days of racing, was mine. This meant but one thing: I was now a marked man.

Not all of the contenders vying for all four deserts in one year were so fortunate. Jimmy Olsen aggravated a nagging injury and was forced to discontinue. It was a stark reminder that even on fresh legs at a very early stage of the race, anything could happen. The contest to complete all four of the desert races in the same year was now a little narrower. Four men had entered, three men remained.

Of course, the racing was only one element of the adventure. To me, the richer experience was running through such a remote and fascinating place. Sandwiched between the Pacific Ocean and the towering Andes Mountains—which create a powerful rain shadow on their leeward side—the Atacama landscape resembled the red planet. In fact, this is the site where the NASA-funded Earth-Mars project was tested.

DAY TWO While rainfall is nearly nonexistent in the Atacama Desert, water is present in certain areas, as I came to learn on the second day of racing. Created by underground springs that percolate to the surface, large bodies of liquid can form along the desert floor. The sun quickly evaporates the water content of these shallow pools, resulting in massive salt flats that stretch as far as the eye can see in every direction.

Running through these salt flats is quite possibly the most perfect form of torture ever devised. Picture tiptoeing across a sharp, brittle field of coral, every step presenting the possibility of breaking through the porous surface whereupon your lower leg is deposited into a salty liquid slurry below.

Wait, it gets better.

Should you break through, on your foot's descent into the steamy saltwater pool, your lower leg gets lacerated by pointed barbs of crusty calcified minerals (effectively simulating rubbing salt on a fresh wound).

Some of the competitors had encountered salt flats in the past and wore sturdy knee-high gaiters to help protect their legs from being slashed. Others, like me, contended with the misery and bloodshed.

It was tough going in Stage 2, and I struggled. The heat was oppressive, and the straps of my heavy pack cut into my shoulders along the neckline. Wanting to minimize weight, I hadn't brought BodyGlide to lubricate potential areas of chafing, so I kept tugging up the collar of my shirt as far as possible in an effort to protect my neck. The fix was only temporary, however, as the shirt material quickly receded below the shoulder strap after only a few short strides. Eventually I gave up and simply allowed the straps to abrade my skin raw. Some battles are not worth fighting.

My performance suffered, and I lost the Yellow Jersey to Rob James.

DAY THREE Sleep continued to elude me. The night air was frigid and the ground lumpy and even colder than the air. All night long I stared wide-eyed at the roof of the tent, unable to progress anywhere close to sleep, no matter how hard I tried. And the harder I tried, the more frustrated I became.

Sunrise on Stage 3 infuriated me. I was angry at the desert, irritated at my body for not functioning more efficiently, and questioning why I had taken on such a ludicrous challenge. In all-out rage, I ran like hell.

Anger can be a powerful energizer. On this day, it set me ablaze. I bounded over rock outcroppings, tore across sandy expanses, and flew up hills. The adrenaline in my system was stratospheric. I hardly ate a piece of food or drank any liquid. My system was in overdrive.

Rounding a long sweeping corner in the course, a small tent city appeared in the distance, signifying the end of Stage 3. Sprinting toward the encampment, I also noticed something peculiar in the distance: rain clouds.

When I arrived at camp, the clouds had moved even closer. I'd finished the day's race a good distance in front of the other runners and thought I might try to sleep for a bit before the tent filled with commotion. As I spread my sleeping bag on the ground, the tent flaps began to rustle. By the time I'd gotten situated and lay down, the impossible happened: It started to rain.

Suddenly, a mighty gust of wind ripped through the camp, sending a massive plume of dust spiraling skyward. The tent began to flutter wildly, the sturdy canvas walls undulating like flimsy rice paper. The steel spikes used to tie down the tents had been driven into the ground with a sledgehammer, yet they were ripped from the earth like toothpicks.

The next thing I knew, I was in orbit. My entire tent was lifted into the sky and was now swirling in the air with the dust and debris like a handkerchief in a windstorm.

The tent and I were hurled downwind; we twisted in flight and landed with a loud scraping noise. Inside, it was utter chaos. It all happened so quickly that there was nothing I could do but shelter my head with my arms in a desperate attempt to protect my skull from the whirling metal tent spikes. I got rolled up inside the tent; my appendages pinned in place.

As quickly as the squall erupted, it passed. I began hearing footsteps of people scurrying around, and muffled voices, but I wasn't sure where I had landed or if anyone knew I was trapped inside. I started calling out, "Help! Help!" to alert someone of my whereabouts.

A voice came back, "Where are you?"

"In here."

There was silence for a moment, then, "In . . . where?"

"In the tent! I'm stuck inside."

They ran over and eventually were able to free me. I'd only suffered minor scrapes and scratches, but the incident shook me to the core. Had something more serious occurred, it could have been grave. We were a long way from a hospital.

DAY FOUR Although I'd won Stage 3, Rob James remained the overall leader. The man was both a champion and a gentleman, and he freely shared with me some of the techniques he used to trim excess weight from his pack, sleep more soundly, avoid being sliced like a tomato by the salt flats, and retain some semblance of hygiene and human decency while not bathing for a week.

This gesture of camaraderie struck me as quite noble. I wasn't trailing too far behind him in the standings and there were a slew of other strong competitors from the United Kingdom, New Zealand, Canada, and Australia close on our heels. Rob's display of graciousness forever solidified him as a hero in my book. The fact that I was able to sleep for a few hours the fourth night because of the advice he gave me—to place a scrap of cardboard under my sleeping bag for warmth—only served to reinforce this sentiment.

DAY FIVE Stage 5 is the notorious "long stage." The distances of the first four days of racing ranged from twenty-four to twenty-eight miles. Stage 5 was more than fifty. It is the day many competitors dread most.

I hadn't formed an opinion yet. Sure, I was trashed from the previous four days of racing, but my pack was considerably lighter since I'd eaten much of my food. I tend to excel at longer distances, so I vowed to keep an open mind during this stage. Everyone, I felt certain, was suffering to some degree; perhaps I was hurting a little less than the rest of the field and could outperform them during this protracted contest of endurance.

When the gun sounded for the start, I went out hard, thinking others might chase me and I could wear them down. They were smarter than that; they let me go.

I led the race the entire day with no one in sight for miles. There were points where I was sure I'd become lost, not spotting any of the small pink flags that marked the course for what seemed like an eternity. Then, magically, one would appear before me.

Hours passed as I ran through the desert alone with no sign of life anywhere. I went into a meditative groove and flowed through the desert landscape, totally immersed in the solitude of my surroundings and awestruck by the grandeur of the desert. I felt small out here, and that invigorated me. There was a primitive energy to the setting, something we rarely experience in our modern concrete world. Out there, running through the desert all alone, the words of Philippe Diole rang true: "Whether one walks, rides a camel, flies, or dives deep into the seas, it is for the sole purpose of crossing a frontier beyond which man ceases to feel himself the master, sure of his techniques, upheld by his inheritance, backed by the crowd. The more powerless he is, the more his spirit permeates his being."

Darkness began replacing light, and still I ran, uncertain how far I'd come and how much farther I still needed to go. It didn't matter; I could run forever and not tire. My heart, lungs, and spirit were free.

Just as the path was darkening to the point where I'd require a headlamp, the finish line emerged. I was neither happy nor sad. It was just an occurrence that signified a change in what I was presently doing; that was all.

I don't even recall going to sleep that night. I slipped off into a deep slumber, without a care or thought. For the first time since arriving in the desert, I slept soundly through the night.

DAY SIX At the start of the final stage of racing, I was presented with the Yellow Jersey. There was clapping and applause and pats on the back. It all seemed presumptive. I was confused. We still had one more day of racing.

Apparently, as they went on to explain, I'd won the "long stage" convincingly, not just making up the time difference Rob had on me, but adding enough buffer that I could walk this final stage at a fast pace and still end up victorious.

The last day of racing is typically short—five or six miles—which is just not enough distance to make up any appreciable time. They had been congratulating me because I had all but won the event.

A group of six of us ran the final stage side by side and crossed the finish line with our hands raised together in a show of unity. All six of us were from different countries, and for me this was the pinnacle of a remarkably transformational experience. Crossing the finish line as a team meant far more to me than winning the race myself. In my eyes, anyone who crossed that finish line was a true champion.

Tintin and Paul also completed the event. Tintin looked pretty good at the finish. Paul was a wreck. He had experienced many problems along the way—from blisters to gastrointestinal distress—and struggled to finish. It took a toll on him. His muscles were atrophied and weak, and his eyes were sullen and withdrawn. Still, deep inside, that magical sparkle of his continued to shine. He might have been beaten, but he wasn't defeated.

The three of us took a group photo under the finish banner. Our next rendezvous would be the Gobi Desert in Central Asia. We had a short couple of months to recover and prepare, and then it was off on another far-flung adventure. We shook hands and vowed to continue the quest to complete the remaining three desert races this year.

Then, just like that, we disappeared into our respective corners of the world.

17.0

Atacama Aftermath

"Prediction is difficult, especially about the future."
—Yogi Berra

THE JOURNEY HOME after the Atacama Crossing was a protracted affair involving multiple bus rides, airline flights, shuttle transfers, taxi trips, security checkpoints, and passport clearances. I arrived back in San Francisco some fifty hours after departing the desert. It was a beautiful clear day in the city, but my head was clouded with the thick fog of a long trip home.

Sifting through the mail at my house, I came upon a letter from the mayor's office. Inside was an official invitation from Mayor Gavin Newsom to carry the Olympic torch on its upcoming passage through San Francisco.

Incredible! Just days after running across one of the most desolate and remote places on earth, I'd be carrying the Olympic flame

through the crowded city streets of San Francisco. The contrast
seemed surreal.

In watching the news that night, however, I came to learn that the
torch run might not be so tame after all. Massive protests had erupted
over China's policies in Tibet and Darfur, and the approaching Beijing
Olympics were the focus of aggressive street demonstrations. During
the torch's recent passage through London and Paris, the situation
had turned violent. Its next stop: San Francisco.

The process of being selected as an Olympic torchbearer had
been a highly competitive one. First, I was nominated by Mayor
Newsom's office. Second, I completed a lengthy application essay.
Finally, I was informed in writing that the committee had offi-
cially selected me. Over the course of that period, the political
situation between the Beijing government and Tibet and Darfur
had escalated to a level that none of us torchbearers could have
ever anticipated. Suddenly, the traditionally peaceful and harmonious process of passing a lighted flame from one Olympic torch
to another was wrought with controversy. In the protests that had
erupted, some demonstrators attempted to snuff out the flame,
even by force, going so far as to attack a handicapped torchbearer
in an effort to do so.

What started as an altruistic dream to carry the Olympic torch
had abruptly become a weighty political decision. Or so it seemed.
When it got right down to it, I ultimately realized that my political
views on the situations in Tibet and Darfur, and my desire to pass the
Olympic flame around the globe in a show of solidarity and unity,
were two completely separate issues. As they rightly should be.

It has long been my position that athletics and sport are a way to bring people together, not divide them. To me, the Olympic torch relay and the Olympic Games are a place of celebration, not a political stage. My decision to carry the Olympic torch came without reserve. Despite my personal feelings on the need for the Beijing government to make positive reform in Tibet, Darfur, and elsewhere, politics simply has no place in this peaceful worldwide event. The Olympic torch symbolizes freedom, unity, and hope. The Olympic torch relay and the Olympic Games must be preserved as a forum for humanity to set aside its differences and rise above the mire of conflict and discord. May the Olympic ideals always shine above all else; for, in doing so, they preserve a glimmer of optimism that as a global community we can somehow realize peace and harmony. Putting out the Olympic flame would squelch this ongoing persuasive message of hope being cast off by its bright light.

No, I would carry the torch. And I would carry it proudly.

• • • •

Security surrounding the torchbearers was intense. While the mayor's office coordinated our movements, the operation involved local, national, and international government agencies and law enforcement bureaus.

They corralled us torchbearers into an undisclosed location in San Francisco to brief us on the day's operation and prepare us for what lay ahead. The torch route had been planned in advance and publicly announced, so we knew the course we would be covering. The briefing was more about the process each of us would follow during our tour of duty, transferring the Olympic flame from one torch to the next.

My family was positioned at the street location of my segment. When the briefing ended, I called my mom from my cellphone. When she answered, there was loud noise and commotion in the background.

"Is everything all right?" I asked.

"There's a lot of protesting going on."

"Are you guys safe?"

"Right now, yes. But there are lots more people arriving every minute."

"Just be careful," I told her. "I'll call you again when we leave the building and begin heading for the start."

They took us from the briefing room down a stark white service hallway and put us into a freight elevator. We went down a couple floors. When the door opened, there was a squadron of policemen awaiting our arrival. They escorted us out a back entrance and ushered us into a large tour bus that was idling outside. It didn't appear any of the protestors knew of our whereabouts, as the streets around us remained calm.

The bus sat idle for quite some time, and a few of us grew anxious. There was a lot of police activity outside the bus, but the bus didn't move. The driver had no answers. He was just doing what he was told.

Suddenly, the bus doors swung open and in came Mayor Newsom.

"Good morning, everybody," he said with his characteristic charm. "We've had a slight change of plans."

Now all of us were sitting on the edge of our seats.

"The first thing I'm going to ask you to do," Mayor Newsom went on, "is turn off your cellphones. It's imperative that nobody on the outside knows our position."

There was restless stirring among us. He continued.

"We've decided to alter our route to avoid the protesters. Everyone will still follow the instructions you were given this morning, we'll just be using a different course. Are there any questions?"

We were all too shocked to respond. The entire scene seemed surreal.

"Okay, have a great run!" And with that, he walked out.

After a moment of pause, the bus erupted with lively conversation. Could this all be true? Were we *really* following a different route? How would we alert our friends and family if we couldn't use our cellphones to call them?

The bus still did not move. The conversations continued and the tension mounted. Our poor families were sitting out there in the midst of a potentially violent situation awaiting our arrival, and we weren't coming! Finally, I asked the bus driver to turn on the radio so we could listen to the news. Almost every station was covering the drama. Then he was given the go-ahead to start moving. Encircled by police cars and motorcycle cops, we began heading down the street.

As we made our way across town, a helicopter joined the security procession from above. Then another . . . then another . . . then yet another. Eventually there was an entire flock of helicopters hovering overhead.

I asked the driver to please turn up the radio so we could hear if the news was reporting anything additional. To our astonishment, they were reporting our exact location! Those weren't police copters overhead, they were news stations broadcasting our position live!

We heard them explaining that we'd just turned down Van

Ness Street and appeared to be heading in the precise opposite direction of the published route.

We sat in paralyzed disbelief listening to the broadcast. Then something very obvious occurred to me. If anyone with a TV, Internet, or a radio knew where we were, why couldn't I call my family and tell them?

I flipped on my cellphone and dialed Julie. "Hon," I screamed into the receiver, "get off the street you're on and hail a cab!"

"Why? We want to see you carry the torch."

"We're going somewhere else!" I barked into the phone. "No time to explain, just hurry. Go quickly! Text me when you're in the cab."

I received her text message not long thereafter and called her immediately. "It appears we're heading for the marina."

"Yeah, I know."

"How?"

"The taxi driver has the radio on." This whole thing was moving too fast for my jet-lagged brain to register all the variables.

"We're heading there now," she told me. "We can see a bunch of helicopters off in the distance and we're going toward them."

The bus arrived at the new designated starting point and the first torchbearers were summoned outside to begin the relay. Other than the loud noise from the helicopters and our surrounding police and security motorcade, the streets were relatively quiet. That all changed quickly, though, as we began the procession of relaying the flame from one torchbearer to the next. Just as my family was listening to the live newscast, so were the protestors who were hunting us down.

The demonstration continued to grow in mass as the succession of torchbearers passed along the flame. My turn was coming up shortly. Just as I was about to call Julie and update her on the predicted location of my segment, I saw her running alongside the bus on the sidewalk outside!

There was my family weaving in and out of protestors. I began banging on the window and yelling at them, but they couldn't hear me. I saw that my daughter, Alexandria, was carrying her cellphone as she ran, so I called her.

"Sweetie, look over at the bus, that's me!" I began waving my hand in the bus window.

"Dad, I can't see anything," she screamed in the phone. "The windows are tinted!"

At that precise moment, the bus door swung open and they announced it was my turn to go. The stretch I would be covering was one of my favorite running spots in the world, along the San Francisco waterfront at the Marina Green. I had pushed Alexandria and Nicholas in a jog stroller down this very path from the time they were born. As I exited the bus, my skin began to tingle.

Once I stepped outside, that feeling disappeared. A posse of bodyguards manhandled me into a semicircle of police who were clad in riot gear. They carried shields in front of them and wore protective facemasks, hunched together shoulder-to-shoulder like the Roman military.

In the mayhem of sensory and emotional overload, time stood still. I flashed to my left and saw Alexandria smiling at me; I turned the other way and saw an agent with a gun in his holster. I heard the cry of a protestor. I watched the previous torchbearer touch the tip of his torch to mine and a magical flame appeared in my hand. I stood there transfixed by it all, unable to process the events that were transpiring in front of me. Then I heard someone yell, "Don't just stand there . . . RUN!"

The human blockade surged forward and I began doing the one thing I knew how to do: run.

The noise was deafening. People hollered my name and shouted at me from all directions. Sirens sounded and the chopping of helicopter rotors whipped through the air. I continued to run.

Cameras pointed my way out of the backs and sides of news vans, supporters waved happily from the sidewalk, and throngs of protestors stumbled clumsily over each other in an attempt to move closer to the flame. All the while, I ran.

Eventually, another torchbearer appeared in front of me. I united the tip of my torch with hers and passed the flame along. The bus door opened again and I was instantly sucked back into the protective vacuum of the vehicle. The last thing I saw was Alexandria, Julie, and my family hugging safely on the grass behind the chaos. I waved through the window, knowing they couldn't see me, but not caring. We had overcome.

• • • •

After numerous fits and starts, the flame eventually made its way successfully to Beijing. Civil unrest would continue to dog the torch relay for the entire distance. Still, nothing could detract from the serendipitous moment my family and I had shared during its passage through our beloved city of San Francisco. The magic of the Olympic flame will burn inside us forever.

18.0

My Toughest Ultra

"If you mess up your children, nothing else you do really matters."
—JACQUELINE KENNEDY ONASSIS

I'M SOMETIMES ASKED what's been my toughest ultra. In truth, it's been raising two kids. At least with an ultra you know what's expected of you, the rules of engagement are clear. There's a starting line and there's a finish line. Make it between the two, you succeed; don't, you fail. Plain and simple. Sure, the space between the two might be daunting and covering that distance might not be easy, but at least you know what's required for success.

Not so with children. With children, the finish line moves around a lot. At times you may think you're moving in the right direction, only to discover that the rules have changed. Nothing is obvious. The only certainty is how easy it is to mess things up. In school, you get the lesson and then take the test; in parenting, you take the test and then get the lesson.

Have I been a good father? To be honest, I really don't know. I certainly have some regrets and wish I had done some things differently; hindsight is always twenty/twenty, I guess. The one thing I can say with one hundred percent certainty, however, is that I've always tried my best.

So just what *do* my kids think of me as a father? Why don't we ask them.

Q&A with Alexandria and Nicholas

Alexandria

Q: Your dad travels frequently; do you miss him?

A: *Yes. But I know that's what he loves to do. We always celebrate when he comes home, so we make up for his being away. Plus, he always texts us pictures from around the world. That's really cool!*

Q: Sometimes you go with him on these journeys; do you enjoy that?

A: *Most of the time. We never get to sleep in, though, so sometimes I get tired. We've been to some great places. Once we got stuck in the middle of the Canadian Rockies; that wasn't very fun.*

Q: What's your best memory with your dad?

A: *There are so many incredible memories with my dad! Seeing him running toward us after finishing the New York City Marathon during the fifty marathon cross-country* *journey stands out. Also, one time he took my friend and me to the top of Bald Mountain to take pictures of the sunset, but we got a late start so he made us run all the way up. It was exhausting, but we made it to the top in time and got some great sunset photos!*

Q: What's your favorite thing to do?

A: *Hang out with my friends. I love photography more than anything and I like capturing life with my camera. I enjoy having dinner with my family every night, even though it's very quick sometimes. I love traveling to new places and exploring, and also going to the beach. Whoops . . . I guess that's more than just one favorite thing.*

Q: Do you want to be a runner?

A: *I enjoy running, but I don't want to make it my career. I don't have the self-motivation for running the way my dad does. I like it for exercise and a way to clear my head, so I'll probably keep it up. But not for a living*

Q: If you could be anything, what would it be?

A: *A photographer. Art's my thing, and photography's my favorite form of art.*

Nicholas

Q: Your dad travels frequently; do you miss him?

A: *Yes, a lot. It's more fun when he's around. Though sometimes it's nice when he's gone because no one bags on me. I can get away with more [laughter].*

Q: Sometimes you go with him on these journeys; do you enjoy that?

A: *A ton! I love to travel. I like meeting different people and trying different foods. Sometimes it's tiring, but I still love to travel with him.*

Q: What's your best memory with your dad?

A: *Racing down the street. We'd go shopping together, and he'd challenge me to a race at every street corner. That was a lot of fun! (Note to reader: When we'd go shopping, I'd run with a backpack and put all of the food inside. When Nicholas refers to "racing down the street," he is talking about on foot, not in a car.)*

Q: What's your favorite thing to do?

A: *Hanging out with my friends. Sometimes we go hiking or go on bike rides, but mostly we just hang out together and go to each other's houses.*

Q: Do you want to be a runner?

A: *No. I mean, I like to run, sometimes. But it's not always my favorite.*

Q: If you could be anything, what would it be?

A: *I don't know. Do I have to? Let me finish sixth grade and maybe I can tell you then.*

19.0

Hotter Than Yesterday

"I have nothing to offer but blood, toil, tears, and sweat."
—**WINSTON CHURCHILL**

LOCALS DUBBED THE Gobi March "the Race of No Return." Ranked number two on Time magazine's list of the "World's Top Endurance Competitions," the second of the 4 Deserts races takes place in the Xinjiang Province of China, in an area closed to foreigners along the ancient Silk Road. Special permits are issued to the competitors—who hailed from twenty-six different countries around the globe—to allow entry into this inaccessible region.

Gobi is the largest desert in Asia. Bordered by the Altai Mountains and Tibetan Plateau, it covers a massive area in China and southern Mongolia. Because it is situated in the rain shadow of the towering Himalaya range, rain-carrying clouds are blocked from reaching the Gobi by the world's tallest peaks, effectively creating an area of almost unimaginable aridness.

In every element, the Gobi is a land of dramatic extremes. Soaring sand dunes abruptly yield to rapidly flowing rivers flanked by spectacular outcroppings of rock and scree that yield to massive expanses of open grasslands. Temperatures can fluctuate by as much as seventy-five degrees during any given twenty-four-hour period and can sometimes oscillate thirty to forty degrees within a single hour. The only certainty out here is that nothing is certain.

The Gobi March was founded in honor of three Christian missionaries, Mildred Cable and two sisters, Francesca and Eva, who began their work in China around the turn of the twentieth century. After more than twenty years, they decided to head northwest—to the Gobi Desert. Many of their colleagues were shocked. In the words of Eva, "Some wrote, saying in more or less parliamentary language, that there were no fools like old fools."

They were undeterred. After traveling for months by ox cart, they arrived at the City of the Prodigals, the last city inside the Great Wall (named for its reputation for attracting criminals). Here they set up a base where they spent winters. The remainder of the year they evangelized, traveling the vast trade routes of the Gobi Desert in Gansu and Xinjiang provinces. They made a point of visiting the lonely, the rejected, and the poorest of the poor, feeding orphans, healing the sick, and educating girls. Along the way, they were assailed by bandits, caught up in local wars, and trapped by periodic blinding blizzards.

Mildred once said: "Only a fool crosses the great Gobi without misgivings." But in the stark landscape, she found wisdom: "In this trackless waste, where every restriction is removed and where you are beckoned and lured in all directions . . . one narrow way is the only road for you. In the great and terrible wilderness, push on with eyes blinded to the deluding mirage, your ears deaf to the call of the seducer, and your mind un-diverted from the goal."

The people who live in the Gobi Desert are a hardy and rugged breed who have learned to survive and endure in this unforgiving land. The men are tanned and strong, the women hardworking and enterprising. The children are bright-eyed and inquisitive, dressed in colorful hand-knitted clothing and wearing ornate mohair beanies with long earflaps adorned by bushy tassels at both ends.

Thirteen distinct indigenous cultures live along the 155-mile Gobi March route, each with a proud heritage and unique way of life. We would experience all of them.

• • • •

My suspicion is that, like me, most of you reading these pages are drawn to extremes. Moderation bores you. You seek challenges and adventures that dwell on the outer edges. The path of least resistance is not a route often traveled.

In reflecting on what compelled me to compete in the 4 Deserts races, and in the Gobi March in particular, it's this attraction toward extremes. The 4 Deserts go beyond just extremes of human endurance—like running for forty-eight hours nonstop on a treadmill. They embody extremes in geography, climate, topography, terrain, and, with the Gobi, culture. To me, it just doesn't get any better.

With all of these elements combined, tell me, does it get any better?

Arriving in the remote outpost of Kashgar, deep in the heart of central Asia, after three days of travel across fifteen time zones, I stepped out of the final airplane flight jet-lagged, sleep-deprived, stiff, dehydrated, and very, very content. Having an affinity for the outer edges, I'd found what I'd been looking for.

The next six days would be a mixture of joy, pain, elation, and agony. We would run through areas rarely seen by outsiders, passing through villages where children lined the course and observed us like we'd emerged from another dimension. Nomads traveled past us on camelback, the entire sum of their worldly possessions warehoused inside small saddlebags. By Western standards, they had nothing. But judging by their look of pride and purpose, it was clear they were far from poor. Far richer than most of us, in fact.

During the course of each day's race, the field thinned, and I frequently found myself running for great distances in complete isolation. Such moments were remarkably purifying. It would have been a mistake to become preoccupied with the fact that this was an athletic contest and not to notice the immense beauty of the land we were traveling through. While I maintained an awareness that this was a race, I tried never to let this detail cloud my vision.

As the days wore on, each night at camp the line for the medic tent grew progressively longer. In crossing the rivers during the day, it was impossible to keep your feet dry. Wet feet combined with hot and rocky desert terrain meant blisters, and many of the competitors were in need of medical attention. Word was that Tintin had blisters the size of grapes covering his toes. His friends said it looked bad, but they had seen him push through much worse. This was his specialty—enduring any imaginable setback and persevering. They weren't worried about him.

My feet had managed to survive relatively unscathed through the first four stages, with the exception of one nagging blister on my right foot, under my big toenail of all places. The pressure had grown steadily more painful each day, the size and girth of the bubble increasing with every footstep. It got to the point where even putting my shoe on in the morning was agonizing.

The tent I shared in Gobi was with a group of Irishmen. Elite marathoners, they had made the transition to multiday racing with consummate attention to detail. Being Irishmen, however, they were also tremendous pranksters and a lot of fun. When one of them suggested an outlandish remedy for my blister, I was suspicious.

After the fourth day of racing, however, I decided to trust him. Day five was the notorious "long stage," and I couldn't imagine enduring the pain through fifty-seven miles of desert hell. He instructed me to use a hollow-point needle—the type used for drawing blood—to drill a hole through the top of my toenail.

"What? You've got to be kidding," I said. He assured me he was not. I did as he told me, slowly boring a perforation through the nail. The very sight of it made me light-headed. Surprisingly, the pain wasn't that bad.

When the needle finally penetrated my toenail completely and reached the inflamed skin below, a gush of purple-blue pus came shooting out the top.

"Now press down on your toenail," he coached.

I did, and more fluid drained out. Miraculously, the pressure and pain were gone!

Not so for Tintin. His troubles continued to escalate. While I made up time during the "long stage," he suffered miserably. His feet became so swollen that the pressure of his shoes made running impossible. So he walked. The going was arduously slow. Eventually even walking became unbearable. Midway through the stage, he was forced to withdraw from the competition altogether. The Gobi Desert had cruelly extinguished his ambition of completing all of the 4 Deserts races. It wasn't the first dream this unforgiving land had quashed, nor would it likely be the last.

Paul Liebenberg fared decently and was able to complete the event, performing better than he had in Atacama, and I placed fourth overall. Four men had entered the 4 Deserts quest, two men remained.

Next stop, the Sahara. Though I would be taking a slight detour along the way.

Prior to accepting the 4 Deserts offer, I'd registered for the 135-mile Badwater Ultramarathon. A couple weeks after the Gobi March, I found myself heading for Death Valley once again.

As many times as I've participated in the Badwater Ultramarathon, it never seems to get any easier. And certainly having Gobi preceding so closely this year didn't make matters any better. My levels of endurance and strength were sufficient going into this year's Badwater, but my legs were still wobbly from the Gobi Desert.

I managed to finish the race—coming in fourth place overall—and continued my Badwater tradition of vowing to *never* run this race again. However, as of the writing of this book, I've amassed eight

Badwater buckles and am preparing to head back to Death Valley in a few weeks for a shot at number nine. Can't stop, won't stop.

As any hardened ultramarathoner can tell you, it gets in your blood. Once the trauma of a punishing race subsides, a renewed restless craving for more surfaces stronger than ever. Recovery? Rest? Who needs it? There'll be plenty of time for that when you're ten feet under. Right now, there's lots of life to get after. Endurance never sleeps . . .

GOBI MARCH

▶ Crossing the finish line in the Gobi Desert with friend Stone Tsang of Hong Kong

20.0

Letters to Karno

"He who undervalues himself is justly overvalued by others."

—WILLIAM HAZLITT

PERHAPS A BETTER title for this chapter would be "I'm Not Worthy," because that's the way I feel. Over the years, I've received tens of thousands of letters, messages, and e-mails from people who tell me that I've had a positive impact on their lives. I am honored.

However, as thankful as I am—and as happy for these individuals as I remain—I've never viewed myself as worthy of such praise. To me, I'm just a runner, no different than any of the folks leaving me these inspiring notes.

Having the moniker "Karno" helps to diffuse some of my discomfort. Karno is an alter ego of sorts, a parallel being who is better suited to be the subject of such admiration. Let him deserve the credit; he is the one who inspires, not me.

In college, I read a book called *Dear Mrs. Roosevelt: Letters to Eleanor Roosevelt*, and it left a lasting impression on me. The book is a collection of nearly two hundred letters written to the first lady during the Great Depression and World War II, a time of incredible unrest and upheaval across the globe. As much as it revealed the compassion and optimism of Eleanor Roosevelt, I found that it revealed the strength and character of the individuals writing to her even more so.

The thought of doing a "letters" chapter came to me as I was preparing to depart on a training run one day with Topher. It was a crisp spring afternoon, and we were planning on doing a loop through Golden Gate Park and out to the beach. As we were lacing up our shoes at my house, the mail slid through the slot and there were a number of fan letters in the pile.

"Look at this," I said, holding one of them up. "I don't even know where they get my address. I'm unlisted."

"Dude, you're making a difference. You're changing the world."

"Microwaveable pizza changed the world. I'm not doing squat."

"You're having more of an impact than you realize, Karno."

"Sure, I've got some pretty cool fans, but look at someone like Brad Pitt."

"Brad Pitt has admirers. You *inspire* people. There's a big difference between admiring someone and being inspired by them."

"I don't know, Toph, I feel like I'm just out there doing what I love, that's all."

"That's why people are so inspired by you."

"It's just running."

"Hey man, you're not afraid to be your own person, and people find that inspiring. You're living your dream. It gives them hope that they can do the same."

"Okay, Gandhi, let's go running."

• • • •

This chapter highlights those incredible individuals who have taken the time and energy to reach out to me with openness and candor.

People sometimes ask if I read all of this correspondence. My answer is an emphatic "Heck yeah!" Where do you think I draw my inspiration?

And now, on to the good part.

FROM KM: "I just wanted to tell you that I threw away my TV last night (at 2:00 in the morning) after finishing your latest book. I had been watching the Olympics and had a 'moment' and decided that I'd rather be doing things myself than watching other people fulfill themselves.

"I, too, have a story. I've lost both my husband and daughter. I thought I would lose my mind, but instead decided to try to find myself. What you write is so true, we have killed our souls with comfort instead of seeking fulfillment and achievement.

"I just wanted you to know what a profound effect you've had on my life. Thank you from the bottom of my heart. I don't know any other way to say it."

FROM CN: "I didn't sleep last night. Yesterday someone gave me a copy of your book. Today I quit my job and started running. I was CEO of the company.

"When I looked in the mirror, I couldn't believe what I'd become. I had dark circles under my eyes, what little hair I had was graying, and my gut was growing larger every day. Your story made me realize how wrong my priorities in life had become. So I resigned, walked out the door, and started running.

"I'm not sure where I'll go. Right now it just feels incredible to be free. My pace is slow, but I know things will improve as the weeks go by.

"This message must sound crazy to you, but thank you for saving my life."

FROM WK: "I certainly don't expect you to remember me and won't be offended if you don't. I had the privilege of running a portion of the Wichita Marathon with you during your Endurance 50 challenge. I was the cross country/track coach from [an esteemed] University who handed you one of our team shirts.

"When I met you, I had long considered myself to be an accomplished marathoner and a respected coach. Still, I never knew what my potential for running could actually be. Then, in November of 2006, I lost one of my closest friends and fellow runners in a tragic airplane accident. From that day forward, I vowed to live life to the fullest and to be a better example to my athletes. Subsequently, with the inspiration from my late friend and the example that you have provided, I have come to grips with my own demons. I have been sober for 372 days as of today. In the process, I have lost thirty pounds, become a dedicated athlete, and have set PRs and won age division awards in virtually every race I have run since the day I met you.

"I just want you to know that while I have never been one to believe in heroes, I now have two—my late friend Mark, who I know continues to run with me every run of every day—and you! As for my running and racing, I know that ultimately we are all mortal, but for the time being, I am not getting older, only faster and tougher . . . like someone else I know!

"Keep it up, Karno, you have inspired more people than you will ever know."

FROM RJ: "My thirteen-year-old son is reading *Ultramarathon Man* and has since tagged you 'that crazy dude.' And my seven-year-old daughter, whom I shared some of the stories from your book with, has since taken a liking to 'hittin' the trails with her old man.' Her words. I love it!"

FROM MT: "I know you've heard it a million times, so I'll make it a million and one: What you do and how you do it has been an unbelievable inspiration to me.

"I don't mean to sound like one of those starstruck fans, but I owe you my life (and if you ever pass through Austin, a pizza, too!)."

FROM ES: "As my son lay dying in the ICU, or living (I couldn't tell which), I read your book and just wanted to thank you for your inspiration. We had just run a half-marathon together the morning I brought him to the hospital. Your book was just what I needed to get me through the night as he was put on an incubator to keep him alive. He is only eighteen but has been diagnosed with an "ultra"-rare condition only less than one in one million have. Go figure, huh? Anyway, thanks. We are praying for a miracle and after reading your book I now believe that miracles can come true."

FROM HE: "I came upon your story two days ago. I didn't think you were a man at all but a machine. That article was the first time I had ever heard of ultramarathoners.

"I immediately went out and bought your book. I finished it in four hours straight, absorbing every detail. I couldn't believe it. You are a machine, but quite human.

"It has always been my life's dream to run a marathon, though I had forgotten my dream over one excuse or another. I am writing you because on the eve of completing your wonderfully written and honest story, I ran my very first half-marathon. Fifty-three times around the track and I would have surely gone for one hundred laps if my friend was not waiting and wondering if I had gone mad. The marathon dream is no longer a question. I have already signed up.

"I have never believed in worshiping other people but you are the first person I feel worthy of such admiration. Your undying dedication to your passion, a passion shared by so many, is just that powerful.

"Thank you for sharing your story and reminding me why I love to run. I hope you'll write more because there is a rare sense of truth and revelation in your words that makes the impossible seem very real and achievable, even by us mere mortals."

FROM LA: "My boyfriend says he loves you. No, LOVES you. Should I be concerned?"

FROM WH: "Perhaps equally as impressive as your running accomplishments is your ability to transcend the artificial impositions of social conditioning. In other words, most people calibrate their perceptions of just what is possible by considering collective past performance. Alternatively, you can make your own mind up about what is or isn't possible—your way! Quite a few of us agree with you deep down, but sadly a rare few translate this into action.

"You have broken down boundaries and in doing so have expanded the realm of what's possible to so many of us, runners and nonrunners alike. Well done and keep going."

FROM JZ: "I have never written a fan letter before, but your story has compelled me. I'm sure you get many of these, so please excuse my inclusion. I just wanted you to know what a profound impact you've had on my wife and me.

"You see, we are training for our first marathon, Marine Corps, and yesterday was our longest run to date, twenty miles. To you this is just a warmup, but to us it was quite daunting. We both survived, barely, and talked about you many times along the way. When things got tough we joked, 'What would Karno do?' to which we always came to the same conclusion, 'He'd keep going!'

"For the first time in my life I think that I can accomplish a marathon, something I never dreamed possible. I've been a lawyer, founder of a successful law firm, recipient of many awards and honors, and benefactor of ungodly prosperity, but nothing is more important to me than finishing this marathon. You have had a profound influence on me, and I just wanted you to know."

FROM PT: "Dear Mr. Karnazes,

"I have long suffered from man boobs. Nothing I've tried has helped, until I read about you. I researched your every word and put your lessons into action. Not only has my problem disappeared, I've lost over twenty kilos. Thank you! If you're ever in the Philippines,

I wish to treat you to some fresh vegetables and fish, foods that are now part of my daily diet."

FROM WS: "Hey Karno,

"A buddy of mine from work and I are huge fans and we came up with WWDD! (What Would Dean Do?) I just ran the NJ Marathon and I wrote on my forearm, WWDD? for inspiration. Well, it worked!

"The weather sucked. It rained nonstop all the way through. I thought about stopping many times, but WWDD? kept me going. Thanks for the inspiration to get me through it. Thanks to you, Boston is now in my future!"

FROM MR: "You came into my life not long ago. I flipped on the TV one rainy evening, glass of Dewars in hand, and you were being interviewed. My life was not going well at the time. I'll spare you the details, but my wife was on crutches from a recent surgery, we were battling a workman's comp claim, my architecture firm was on the brink of closing its door because of the poor economy, and I had just about lost faith that things would ever improve. At sixty years old, prospects for the future were dim.

"The words you spoke during that interview changed everything. I promptly bought a copy of your book on Amazon and it has been the single best investment of my life. No longer do I see obstacles, I only see ways to overcome them.

"Our life has turned around dramatically. We are quickly resolving many of the issues we were faced with and my firm has landed a handful of new contracts. For the first time in years, I have hope! And it's all on account of a shift in my attitude. We embraced a motto back when I served: 'Improvise, Adapt, Overcome.' Thanks for reminding me to always be true to those words."

FROM LT: "I want to run a marathon when I turn twelve. Is that okay?"

FROM BR: "I'm in my seventies and have started running. I love it! I want to run a marathon, is that okay?"

FROM CI: "I like to run, but I don't want to run a marathon. Is that okay?"

FROM LH: "You will not remember me, but we crossed paths as you wound your way marathoning through the various states. I waited with my three-year-old triplets along the course to root for you. I told them to cheer, 'Go, Dean, Go!' which was quickly changed by them to, 'Go Dingo Dean!'

"It was a wonderful interaction that I wrote about in my journal later that day: I don't know the *man*, but I am familiar with the *legend*. And I don't know his motives, but I want to believe he runs for that child within each of us. That same child who once told us, 'You can jump farther than the moon and run faster than the stars.' That same child who told me this morning, 'Your best years of running have yet to come.' And that same dreamful child who I now fully believe.

"Success to you, Dingo Dean, for your success is our success."

FROM SD: "Karno,

"Your quote, 'Run when you can, walk when you have to, crawl if you must; just never give up,' inspired my buddy Leo and I to do just that. Working with a group of engineers at Columbia University and through the help of the GM Polymer Company and TempurPedic Mattresses, we had two pairs of specialized kneepads designed for our attempt at setting the new Guinness Book world crawling record. We crawled 32.26 miles in forty-five straight hours, breaking the existing record by over a mile! In the process, we raised $18,000 for the Elizabeth Glaser Pediatric AIDS Foundation. Thank you for the inspiration to crawl further."

FROM SH: "There's an element of the flat-out 'going for it' in your story that people really love. Not just giving it your all in a race, but pushing into that unknown place of life, becoming an outsider instead of a guy in an office. Essentially, everyone wants that, I think, whether they go after it or not."

My response to that final comment: Definitely choose to go after it!

21.0

Sahara Sirens

"You will come to the Sirens first; they bewitch any mortal who approaches them."

—ULYSSES IN HOMER'S *THE ODYSSEY*

EARLY BIBLICAL TRAVELERS reported encounters with angels and demons while crossing the Sahara. They heard strange, inexplicable sounds and saw huge figures dancing across the dunes. Stage 3 of the Sahara Race was a surreal odyssey of that order.

Having navigated along miles of twisting and turning sandstone chasms, I'd become well separated from any of the other competitors when I came over a ridge and encountered a massive plane of deep crimson sand that stretched to the horizon. A procession of small course flags dotted the smooth surface in a single-file line until they tapered off out of sight into the distance. I knew that the flags would eventually lead me somewhere, but where I did not know.

As I ran, temperatures began creeping upward. Each day of racing the temps had gotten progressively warmer, and today was the hottest yet, easily cresting one hundred degrees Fahrenheit. The temperature gauge on my wristwatch read 114 degrees, but it was likely reading a few degrees higher than the actual temperature because of the additional heat being cast from my body. It was probably 110. However, it was still only 11:00 A.M. The upcoming midday heat would likely be five to ten degrees warmer.

I was wearing my desert suit: a white top, highly breathable shorts, gaiters over my ankles to help prevent sand from entering my shoes, and a long-billed white cap with legionnaires flaps to protect my neck from the scorching rays of the sun. But even with this protective and lightweight gear on, the insulated cushioning of my backpack became wickedly hot.

As I ran each night, the shoulder straps, waist belt, and backing of the pack were covered in a crusty white salt from my dried perspiration, and each day this salt would be reabsorbed by the wetness of the day's sweat, making the buildup grow larger and more concentrated each night.

Great waves of heat rose from the desert floor, creating a 360-degree rippling mirage. The ceaseless plateau became disorienting. A slight breeze stirred the sand, creating a fine ground-level fog of desert dust that obscured the horizon. The sky and ground all took on the same monotone hue. I turned back to see if anyone was behind me. No one. When I swung my head forward, vertigo caused me to stumble and nearly fall over. I knew that the ground I ran on was flat, but I couldn't discern whether there were slight rises and depressions in the surface. In the swirling dust, the junction of where the earth ended and the sky began had blended, earth and sky becoming one and the same.

A more savage blast of hot wind whipped across the desert floor in front of me, sending an enormous twist of sand and dust spiraling skyward. The twirling column moved eerily across the desert in an erratic zigzag pattern before evaporating mystically into the sky.

More of these whorls began to materialize, some near and some far away. Blurring plumes of desert heat rose off the ground, which distorted and deformed the more distant spirals, giving them the appearance of disfigured leviathans lurching awkwardly across the desert floor.

It was nearly impossible to get a solid look at these bizarre figures dancing across the desert floor as the superheated air stung my eyes and the blowing debris clouded my vision. Perhaps there really were demons out here, as the early biblical accounts had reported.

After several hours of running along this haunted plane, an abrupt variation appeared in the distance. From where I was, it was difficult to ascertain its height, but as I came closer it became clearer. I looked up at a five-hundred-foot-tall wall of golden-brown sand. With temperatures hitting 110 degrees, I began to scale the monster. It was hellish: With every forward step my foot was swallowed by a sinkhole of burning hot sand.

Along the ascent, my progress came to a near standstill at several points. As I crawled upward on all fours, the unstable sand gave way underneath, and I slid backward to where I'd begun, if not farther down. Beads of sweat dripped from my forehead and a gritty talc coated my teeth. There was no way of rinsing this soot from my mouth; I'd run out of water long ago.

The dunes stretched on for miles. Why they had formed at this particular juncture, and how they were able to accumulate so substantially without being blown flat by the incessant desert winds, was a total mystery.

When I reached the top of the first sandy summit, I proceeded along the narrow ridgeline that formed the apex of the peak. Steep drop-offs flanked both sides of this narrow sliver of sand, and stepping off the centerline in either direction made me slip downhill, further slowing my progress and requiring the expenditure of life-robbing energy.

Taking a straight line would have been a shorter route than weaving atop the slender crest, as I was doing. But to do so would have required dropping down and then climbing back up the sides of these towering dunes, which would involve considerably more physical effort. A straight line might be the shortest distance between two points, but it's not necessarily the shortest amount of time (or the least amount of strain). Conserving energy was more important than shaving distance.

When camp finally emerged in the distance, my energy reserves had all but been depleted. I made my way wearily toward the small speck in the distance, waves of heat still rising from the late-afternoon desert floor. The thought of another freeze-dried meal repulsed me, but there was no other choice. For dessert, I had one remaining stick of gum. That is all I had to look forward to.

The camp seemed unusually barren and desolate when I arrived. Except for the two individuals recording my finish time, there was no one else around. The interior temperature of my canvas tent was unbearable, so I decided to try finding somewhere more comfortable to relax. I hiked over a small crest of sand behind the makeshift tent city and dropped down the backside of a dune. From here, there was nothing in sight but miles and miles of empty desert.

I lay down on my back. The dune I rested upon pointed away from the sun, so the sand was refreshingly cool against my bare skin. I closed my eyes and immediately slipped off to sleep.

When I awoke, I heard a peculiar humming noise somewhere off in the emptiness. At first I thought it could be the distant whine of a jet engine flying overhead, but there were no planes to be seen. I lay motionless on my back, scanning the sky from horizon to horizon. Nothing. Come to think of it, I hadn't seen an airplane this entire week. I began wondering if maybe I hadn't just made up the sound.

But there . . . there it was again. Faint and fleeting, to be sure, but a noise nonetheless. I tried to listen more intently, but the sound was elusive. The pitch sounded increasingly like the high notes of a pipe organ. It reverberated throughout the dunes and it was impossible to figure out from which direction it was originating. Then, strangely, it tapered off completely, leaving an eerie silence. What had produced the noise?

I surveyed the dunes but could only see great mounds of sand in every direction. In the ear-ringing stillness, I started again to question whether I had really heard anything at all.

Then, there it was again. Obscure and ephemeral, but legitimately present from all that I could tell. It was the most unforgettable noise I had ever heard, haunting and otherworldly, like a chorus of angels crying off in the heavens.

Returning to camp, I asked someone about it. "Noise?" they said. "I didn't hear anything."

Had I dreamed the whole episode? I was certain I'd heard a ghostlike hymn, though perhaps it was just an auditory illusion brought on by exhaustion, dehydration, and severe sleep deprivation.

• • • •

Each day crossing the Sahara grew warmer and more intense. My position in the standings at the end of Stage 4 was not as good as I'd hoped, but the heat and brutality of the previous four days had taken a heavy toll on some of the racers ahead of me, and I was able to once again make up a substantial time deficit on the fifth day of racing, the "long stage." A particularly wicked one-hundred-kilometer (sixty-two-mile) ordeal across multiple terrains and settings, I spent much of the day running with the eventual event winner, Ryan Sandes of South Africa.

After so many days of running through the desert alone, it was refreshing to run with a partner. Ryan was just a kid in his twenties, though he possessed a wisdom beyond his years. As the day wore on, we spoke honestly and without superficial clichés. We were both growing weary, and this state of exhaustion opened our dialogue even further. I love interacting with people when they're most exposed, when every layer of pretension and vanity has been stripped away and strewn along the pathway. The ultramarathon doesn't build character, it reveals it. It is here that you get an honest glimpse into the soul of an individual. Every insecurity, every character flaw is open and on display for all to see. No communication is ever more real, no expression ever more honest. There is no hiding behind anything; the ultramarathon is the great equalizer. Every movement, every word spoken and unspoken, is radiant truth. These are the profound moments of human interaction I live for.

Toward the end of the stage we'd depleted our water supply. Once night fell, we wore headlamps to navigate through the remaining course. Knowing we were nearing the finish and would be alloted our daily ration of water soon, Ryan reached into his backpack and popped a handful of electrolyte capsules in his mouth. He swallowed them whole without water.

We soon crossed the finish line of Stage 5 together as the co-winners. A small group gathered around to congratulate us. Ryan was going to say something and all eyes turned to him. Instead, he sneezed. Out of his nose and mouth shot a fine mist of sodium, potassium, magnesium, and chloride (i.e., the contents of the electrolyte capsules). The powder came streaming out of each nostril and swirled around his head and face. In the light of our headlamps, he looked like a fire-breathing dragon.

We all had a great laugh over that one. It was one of those immortal race moments you cherish for years.

The finish line on the final day of racing was at the base of the towering Giza Pyramids. It was a spectacular setting and a picturesque ending to one crazy race. I saw Paul Liebenberg at the finish and he looked pretty darn good, which was unusual. I'd kept an eye on him during the first two races of the 4 Deserts and especially during this third race of the series. To be honest, I was surprised—and incredibly impressed—that he'd made it this far. At the end of each stage of racing he looked completely doomed; every time I saw him, I was convinced he would drop out. Yet here he was, standing proud at the finish of the third race in the series.

Paul is so filled with passion that he has the uncanny ability to leave every last molecule of effort out on the racecourse. He has just one speed: full throttle. This is a dangerous approach in multiday racing, as any single day of huge output can leave you destroyed for the next. But I admired his remarkable resilience. I've never seen anyone lay it all on the line like Paul does.

We toasted with a glass of champagne at the awards ceremony that evening. Ryan won the event, and I was runner-up. We collected our trophies and headed to the airport for the long journey home. The next meeting place for Paul and I would be Antarctica. After spending a week running across the Sahara, the idea of frostbite sounded rather appealing.

• • • •

Upon my return, I would read a story in the *New York Times*: "Secrets of the Singing Sand Dunes." Scientist have explained this phenomenon of singing sand dunes as avalanches in the sand that create a loud—up to 115 decibels—deep hum that can last several minutes. Perhaps those sounds I heard out there in the Sahara may have been real after all.

The Best Race
of My Life

"The only one who can tell you 'You can't' is you. And you don't
have to listen."

—NIKE

IT'S PROBABLY CLEAR by now that I live for adventure.
The more intense, the more remote, the harsher, the better. I've now
raced and competed on all seven continents, twice over.

So it might come as a surprise when I tell you that my favorite race
of all time wasn't a hundred-mile competition through the mountains,
nor a six-day trek across the desert, nor running fifty consecutive
marathons in fifty states. It was a 10-K. Yep, a mere 6.2 miles.

Allow me to explain why.

My first priority in life is always my family. They take precedence
over all else. It's just who I am; it's how I'm hardwired. A proud father
and husband, nothing is more important to me than my family.

That said, I have never pushed running on my two children, fearing the proverbial backlash. If Alexandria and Nicholas wanted to run, that's great. If not, that's their prerogative and I'll love them regardless.

Thus far, neither of them has shown a particular interest in running. They've accompanied me on many of my marathons and ultramarathons, so I know they've been exposed to my antics from day one. But there just doesn't seem to be much interest on their part.

Therefore, you can imagine my astonishment when Alexandria approached me two weeks before her tenth birthday and informed me that she wanted to run a 10-K with me to celebrate the occasion. At first, I wasn't sure how to react. Was she doing this just to appease me, or was this something she really wanted to do for herself? She insisted it was something she wanted to do, and when the day came she seemed as excited as ever to take up the challenge.

When the gun went off and the race began, she darted out at breakneck speed. I knew such an approach was imprudent because one could only hold such an aggressive pace for a short duration, and the toll it could potentially take during the latter stages of the race might be disastrous. Still, I fought back my fatherly impulse to counsel her and, frankly, did all I could to keep up!

By the halfway point, her initial vigor had begun to wane. Running three miles at such a fast pace had left her exhausted. As a father, it was tough to see my daughter so worn out when I could have advised her to slow down and take it easy in the first few miles to help preserve some of her energy for the latter stages. I thought it was an important lesson for her to learn for herself.

Approaching the five-mile mark, the cumulative effects of running, along with the sheer number of minutes on her feet, were really starting to show. She huffed and puffed and struggled to maintain her focus. Things were not looking good. I'd never seen her so worn out before, and it hurt me. I couldn't allow this to continue.

Just as I was about to tell her how incredibly proud I was of her for having the courage to try, and to congratulate her on being able to run five miles, she turned to me and said, "Dad, I'm going to make it."

Never before have I seen such grit and determination to persevere in a young child. She put her head down, let out an audible grunt, and charged into the abyss with unflinching resolve.

People along the course were in total disbelief, as was I. She was a woman on a mission, entirely focused on the task at hand, pumping her arms and thrusting her legs boldly forward with every stride. Spectators cheered for her and applauded wildly as she bounded by.

Me? Forget about it, I was a complete mess. I tried my best to choke back the tears, but finally gave in to my emotions. I was a sobbing child, huge tears running down both cheeks, completely unable to retain my composure no matter how hard I tried.

As we rounded the final corner and the end came into focus, she issued her final tear-wrenching dictum. "Daddy," she said, "give me your hand. I want to hold it when we cross the finish together."

I did as she requested and we burst across the finish line as a team. People rushed over to her and began offering aid and assistance. "I'm fine," she told them. "Really, I'm fine." To be honest, it was me who needed help. I'd come completely unraveled. I've crossed deserts on foot, run over towering mountains, forged raging rivers, but nothing has ever impacted me like the sight of that little girl refusing to give up. It was the most glorious moment of my life.

The memory of Alexandria and me crossing that finish line together has replayed in my mind on countless occasions. No matter how many trophies I win, no matter how many records I set, no matter how many distinctions I earn, nothing will ever top that moment.

Alexandria, my sweet child, thank you for providing dear ol' Dad with that wonderful gift. You may choose to never run again, but you will always have the heart of a champion in my eyes.

23.0

SOS

"Beyond 50 degrees south there is no law, beyond 60 degrees south there is no God."

—Early Polar Explorers

ANTARCTICA IS THE grand finale of the 4 Deserts races and where the overall series champion is determined. In order for a racer to qualify for this event and be eligible for the overall crown, he must have competed in the preceding three events of the series: Atacama, Gobi, and Sahara (though not necessarily in the same year, as Paul and I were attempting to do). Most of the other athletes vying for the overall crown had spent several years on the process, competing in one, or perhaps two, of the other three races during a particular calendar year. The overall series victor is determined by calculating who has the lowest cumulative points from all four of the races.

Going into this final event, my prospects for winning the overall series crown looked fairly promising. I had a total of seven points (first place in Atacama, fourth in Gobi, and second in Sahara). The next closest racer had over twenty points. Still, this was Antarctica. Anything was possible.

To get to the frozen continent, we would be sailing from the tip of South America, departing from the southernmost city in the world: Ushuaia, Argentina. We would need to spend three days navigating across the notorious Drake Passage, long considered one of the most treacherous waterways in the world. It is a rough and dangerous crossing, and because of the surfer's ear condition I developed from many years of catching waves, I am highly susceptible to seasickness. With a patch of transdermal scopolamine medication stuck behind my ear, we pulled out of port.

Already south of latitude 40, the so-called "roaring forties," we would pass through the "furious fifties" and into the foreboding "screaming sixties," a place so savage and sinister that many early sailors refused to journey there, considering it godless.

One of my favorite stories of all time is that of Ernest Shackleton's ill-fated Antarctic expedition in the vessel aptly named *Endurance*. The posting he used to recruit men for this legendary journey read:

---

* MEN WANTED *

For Hazardous Journey. Small Wages, Bitter Cold, Long Months of Complete Darkness, Constant Danger, Safe Return Doubtful.

Honour and Recognition in Case of Success.

The irony of our boat trip was that the seas remained glassy calm. We began calling the deadly passage "Lake Drake." Still, I kept the scopolamine patch on. I'd been warned how quickly and unpredictably things could change. I wasn't about to take any chances.

Antarctica is the coldest, driest, and windiest place on earth. The coldest temperature ever recorded, a life-zapping minus 126.8 degrees Fahrenheit, was recorded here. Unlike the other three races, we would not be required to carry all our food and supplies this time. We would be staying on the main ship at night and then transferring to shore each morning on smaller Zodiac boats for the racing. We still needed to carry a pack with mandatory gear—a down sleeping bag, food for the day, a safety lamp, a multitool knife, a compass, a neoprene facemask, extra clothing, a hydration system, and a variety of other items—but the overall weight of the pack used in Antarctica was less than during the other desert races because it was just one day's worth of provisions versus one week's.

The first day of racing was an incredible challenge. The snow in Antarctica presents a vexing surface to run on. Slogging through knee-deep powder is like trying to find your footing in a tub of Styrofoam pellets. Not only does your foot sink up to the knee, once you're immersed in the frigid void, there seems to be no bottom to push off from.

I wasn't the only one experiencing difficulties; the snow was proving troublesome for all of the competitors. In spite of slow going, at the end of the day I'd managed to capture the Yellow Jersey. I had run on Antarctica before—once completing a marathon to the South Pole—so I had some prior experience dealing with these tricky surface conditions.

What I found most captivating during the first day's event were the penguins. Such curious little creatures! Not having encountered humans before, they weren't intimidated by our presence in the least and would sneak up behind you like a cat. At the interior of Antarctica, where I'd been before, nothing could survive. But these coastal regions were teeming with wildlife.

Once back from shore and loaded onto the main boat, we pulled up anchor and started heading for our next destination. Weather conditions abruptly changed and the seas grew angry. We were told it was going to get rough. I felt queasy almost immediately, so I slapped another "scop" patch behind my ear and waited for the drug to take effect.

Supper that night was not pleasant. Desert crown contender James Elston of the UK commented, "Boycotted dinner, felt sick. If I had eaten, my stomach would have boycotted dinner right back out."

I couldn't eat either, but at least the magic of the drug began to alleviate my nausea. I lay in my cramped, dark quarters being thrashed about. It was dank and claustrophobic, and I wanted nothing more than to be safely on land, preferably somewhere warm and tropical. Dream on.

When we arrived at our designated location the next morning, I didn't remember a thing from the prior night's journey and large blocks of yesterday seemed missing, too. It was a spaced-out feeling, but I attributed it to the fact that the twenty-four-hour sunlight had messed with my body's natural circadian rhythm.

Stage 2 began, and I charged confidently out to the lead in my Yellow Jersey. The course climbed up a steep incline and then down a decline that veered sharply to the right at the bottom. When I hit the corner I went flying, landing on my face in the snow.

This seemed strange. The surface hadn't seemed too slippery, certainly not slick enough to send me toppling. So why had I fallen?

I stood up and brushed off the snow. When I resumed forward progress, I started seeing stars. My stride became progressively more wobbly and erratic. No matter how hard I pushed, my heart rate would not elevate. My legs felt heavy and unstable, like an elephant that had been hit with a tranquilizing dart. Finally, I was forced to stop and sit down.

Other racers began filing past. They were concerned and asked if I was okay. I just smiled and waved them on, trying to catch my breath. Soon the entire field had passed. It was a horrific day of racing. I spent most of it sitting in the snow watching the penguins.

On board that night, I spoke to the medical doctor. He suspected that I may have contracted a virus back on the mainland in Ushuaia where we had stayed for a few days before embarkation, but he wasn't entirely sure. He said it was okay for me to race the next day, but he wanted to continue monitoring me.

The next day wasn't any better. I was out of it, in a complete haze. Still, I needed to participate in the race to remain a contender for the overall crown. A DNF (did not finish) now, after making it this far, would seem ill-fated. But I couldn't see how I would be able to continue in my current state.

Instead of contemplating the ramifications of failure, which was demoralizing, I decided to take action and do what I could. Life is a series of obstacles and setbacks; *living* is overcoming them. I couldn't run, so instead I walked. My progress was painstakingly slow, but it was forward momentum nonetheless. Sometimes the key to getting to where you want to go is simple: Keep going.

It began to snow lightly, and I kept walking. The natural surroundings were stunning. Massive fjords jutted out into the sea, the water surrounding them a dazzling aquamarine. Penguins frolicked, racing streamlined through the water like little mammalian torpedoes.

An athlete from Germany came up beside me and we began walking together and admiring the picturesque setting. We talked along the way. Turned out, he had experienced a similar malaise. He asked if I had ever worn the patch before. I explained that I hadn't but was very prone to seasickness. Besides, I had taken it off after making the Drake crossing. He told me his symptoms went away after he took his patch off and suggested I do the same. *Ah!* I mumbled. I'd entirely forgotten that I'd put on another patch to contend with our first night's inter-Antarctica voyage and had failed to remove it after we arrived in port.

I reached behind my ear and pulled the thing off, thanking him. Good riddance, I thought. At least now I wouldn't have a foreign substance coursing through my system.

Removing it solved the problem. On the morning of Stage 4 I was back to feeling myself. I'd moved down in the Antarctica race rankings but progressively worked my way back, winning the day's racing and closing the gap that had opened over the past two days. Paul Liebenberg had been racing extraordinarily well; he was in first place in Antarctica. Behind him was James Elston of the UK, then Evgeniy Gorkov of Russia, Carlos Prieto of Spain, and Nicola Benetti of Italy. The standings in Antarctica were now tight; I trailed

Evgeniy slightly. As for the overall 4 Deserts crown, I still maintained a comfortable lead.

On the morning of the fifth day, the long stage, I had a renewed fire. My legs felt fresh and rested, and I finally felt mentally astute. This was going to be my day, I decided.

It wasn't. The fifth day was sheer mayhem. As we motored toward our landing spot, the wind began to increase. By the time we'd made it around the corner of the ice mass and gotten into our landing position, we had a fresh gale in our face. Instead of running for the trophy, it was time to run for cover. Problem was, in the Drake Passage there isn't any.

Our boat spent the next three days being tossed about like a cork in a washing machine. There was only one place to go, back to mainland South America, and it was a harrowing journey. Hurricane-force winds whipped the seas into a frothy white cauldron of churning waves and ice blocks.

Mercifully, we made it back safely. A research vessel behind us wasn't so lucky. A dramatic rescue effort was launched from Argentina to save the crew.

The Antarctica race had come to a safe, though somewhat anticlimactic, conclusion. Paul was pronounced the event winner, as the standings through Stage 4 stood. While it would have been nice for the event to have played out, I was happy to see Paul on the podium. He had worked exceptionally hard to make it this far, sacrificing and suffering so much. His recognition was well deserved. He and I became the first two people to ever complete all of the 4 Deserts races in a single year, and it hadn't been easy. Then again, what in life that's worthwhile ever is?

With my final placing in Antarctica, I was crowned the 2008 winner of the 4 Deserts Championship. The race organization threw an awards celebration in my honor in San Francisco, as was tradition for the overall title winner. We sat in a swank downtown restaurant and the waitstaff fussed and fretted over us. The scene seemed strangely juxtaposed against the raw and inhospitable places I'd been earlier that year: freezing my ass off on the tent ground in Atacama, eating dehydrated porridge out of a bag in the middle of the Gobi Desert, hallucinating in the Sahara, and nearly being capsized in the frozen waters off Antarctica.

As the evening drew to a conclusion and we said our good-byes, I thought about what an incredible journey it had been. Who would have ever thought that my life would have taken such an unexpected course? In the words of those legendary Bay Area rockers, *"What a long, strange trip it's been . . . "*

During the 4 Deserts races, along with the help of my sponsor, The North Face, we were able to raise sufficient funding for the Blue Planet Foundation to provide a lifetime's worth of clean and safe drinking water for 165 families worldwide. In the desert, clean drinking water is a priceless commodity.

24.0

Forty-Eight Hours of Chafing

"Boldly going nowhere."
—BUMPER STICKER SPOTTED IN RUSH-HOUR TRAFFIC

CHAFING IS BAD, as any runner can tell you. Chafing on national television—in front of an audience of millions—is, well, horrendous. Compound the chafing with extreme exhaustion and severe sleep deprivation, and potentially life-altering decisions can be made with reckless abandon. How did I find myself in such a predicament? Here's what went down.

I had no idea what to expect when the *LIVE! with Regis and Kelly* show first contacted me. They asked me to appear on their "Week of Records" program, luring me to attempt a new Guinness world record on live TV. It sounded like an incredible challenge. Just one small detail seemed a tad unsettling: They asked that I run for forty-eight hours nonstop on a treadmill placed inside the lobby window of the ABC-TV studios in downtown Manhattan, with a live webcam documenting my every movement the entire time. Beyond that, it was business as usual.

I flew in from San Francisco the day prior. The setup amazed me. A platform—actually, a stage—had been erected in the lobby of the studio behind huge glass windows right on the corner of Columbus and Sixty-seventh. On the deck were two parallel treadmills set up side by side. This virtual hamster wheel inside a fishbowl would be my home for the next two days.

How did I train? I didn't, really. I despise treadmills; hadn't stepped foot on one in over a year. I would rely almost entirely on my weekly outdoor running to prepare for the challenge. The previous world record of 240 miles in forty-eight hours on a treadmill seemed hugely unattainable, particularly since I had no inherent passion for such equipment. Still, I couldn't refuse a challenge. "Stupid is as stupid does," Forrest Gump said.

I slept little that night. I was terrified. What would happen to me over the next two days? What had I gotten myself into this time?

The *LIVE! with Regis and Kelly* show moves quickly. Seconds matter on national television. Every moment is scripted and choreographed, yet there is a certain frenetic haphazardness to the way situations play out. Stakes are high, exacerbating the intensity.

I stood on the treadmill closest to the window when Regis and Kelly came walking around the corner, surrounded by people giving them last-second instructions, touching up Kelly's makeup and straightening Regis's jacket. The scene had a surreal quality. Then I heard "Roll camera one!" and suddenly it was very real.

The gossip magazines portray Kelly as a ditzy blonde, though she is anything but. She asked intelligent questions, seeking insight, genuinely curious about where my head is at the moment. She was intrigued and captivated by it all.

Regis, on the other hand, seemed a bit taken aback. "So, you plan to run forty-eight hours straight?" he asked, less to inform the millions of viewers than to hear it for himself. I nodded in affirmation.

"Okay, Dean," he said. "Get ready." The large crowd went silent. "On your mark, get set . . . GO!" the two of them chanted mechanically.

Teleprompters read, "Applause! . . . Applause! . . . Applause! . . . " The audience complied and clapped and cheered. Stagehands crowded sheepishly in the backdrop, craning for a view.

I looked down at the controls and pushed a couple of buttons on the display panel. The belt began to move. I put one foot in front of the other and started running. The folly had begun.

• • • •

Within minutes the lobby grew quiet. The cameras were gone, the stars and the audience had moved inside the *LIVE!* set, and the fanfare had entirely dissipated. Beyond the metrical slapping of my feet on the treadmill, the ABC lobby was calm. It was 9:40 A.M. in Manhattan.

The clock started ticking when the gun was fired and it would not stop for forty-eight hours. What I did in between now and then was my business. I could sleep, change clothing, use the bathroom, whatever. The record is about miles covered. That's all that counted. If you're not on the treadmill running, you're wasting precious time. Thus, there was constant pressure to forge onward, no matter how exhausted or fatigued you became.

I ran for the first six hours without a break. My assigned "handler," as the show's producers referred to him (his actual name was Mike), told me about last year's Week of Records, when he was assigned to an opera singer attempting to sing for twenty-four hours straight. He had a horrible voice, Mike explained, and all he asked for was greasy chicken wings. "He'd take brief breaks in between notes and take quick bites. I must have ordered takeout a dozen times."

During those first six hours, I consumed nothing at all, afraid that eating or drinking would cost me precious time in the bathroom. Actually, the awkward fact that observers would be following my bathroom patterns weighed more heavily on me than the time I would lose relieving myself.

Right when I was feeling the overwhelming urge to go, Kelly bounded in, dressed in running attire, perky and energetic. She is one of the hottest numbers on television and in incredible shape. "Can I run with you, Dean?" she asked.

We began running on the parallel treadmills, and I did my best to suppress the mounting bladder pressure. She wanted to talk, and I feared a series of numbingly naive questions and mindless chitchat. Instead, she was intelligent, engaging, witty, empathetic, and perceptive. Whether by briefing or firsthand research, she knew about me and my story.

I, on the other hand, knew almost nothing about her. Suddenly I was the airhead. I don't follow tabloids or gossip magazines, where she is a frequent fixture, and I never took the time to read her bio. I didn't expect to be interested in her. It was me casting stereotypes. The woman running next to me was impressive, not only with her beauty and athleticism—clicking off eight-minute miles with barely a pant!—but even more so with her authentic inquisitiveness and sincere quest for insight and understanding. I was unexpectedly starstruck.

"Regis thinks all of these records are trickery," she told me. "Like none of this stuff is really that difficult. Stunts, you know."

I nodded at her breathlessly, trying to keep up with her pace.

"I'm glad you're here." She bade me farewell after an hour and left to pick up her children from school. At long last, an opportunity for that potty break.

When I returned from the bathroom, the calls started coming in to my cellphone perched on the control panel. "Dude, was that Kelly running next to you? She's hot!"

My friends are idiots. Though I'm even dumber. The phone was on speaker. Everyone in the room heard that comment.

Anyone with a computer anyplace in the world could watch me live for two days straight. It was like *The Truman Show* run amok. If they knew my cellphone number, they could tell me all about it, fill me in, because all I saw from my vantage point was this little marble eyeball staring transfixed upon me.

Regis came strolling by on his way out the door. He inspected me, looking at the treadmill deck spinning and at my pumping arms and thrusting legs. I thought he might be beginning to believe there was less trickery and stunt work in what I was doing, and more honest-to-goodness hard work.

"You look terrific so far," he said. "I'll try to stop by after dinner."

He lives in the building across the way, I am told, along with Howard Stern and a host of other celebrities. This made me feel even more out of place. These people are mega media stars, and here I was running half-naked in the lobby of the office building across from their residence.

Why was I doing this? I don't like being on display. In fact, I like nothing more than to run all night by myself. There's a weird voyeuristic element to it. Exposing myself like this is my biggest horror, but in doing so I felt strangely liberated. I confronted my fears firsthand and in doing so I was, in a way, set free.

Regis stopped in after dinner. "You're still running," he said, perplexed by the fact that while he has been going about his usual routine all day, I have been grinding away on a treadmill.

"Yep," I said, "and I'll be here tomorrow morning when you come back to work."

This seemed to dislocate his sensibilities. He looked up at me, befuddled, almost cross-eyed. Good thing I didn't mention that not only would I be here tomorrow morning but, body willing, the next morning, too. That might have thrown him into a total tailspin.

"All right, Dean, I'll get some sleep for the both of us," he offered.

• • • •

It was approaching midnight. Outside, a young man had taken up residence on the street corner. It was hard to discern whether he was a beggar, homeless, or just interested in what was going on inside. He sat with his back propped up against a street sign and a blanket wrapped around his legs, not seeming to pay much notice to the people walking past him. His blond hair was a bit matted, but he appeared bright-eyed and in good physical shape. He glanced in my direction periodically, though I couldn't tell if he was watching me or not.

There had been a nonstop torrent of commotion and activity all day, and I'd been answering questions nearly continuously. With nightfall, I was hoping to focus, to get back inside my own head. It was not to be.

A new shift of workers entered the building, fresh and inquisitive. I cringed at having to answer more of the same questions, but they were enthusiastic and intrigued. Some told me I have inspired them to get active, to start exercising. I wanted to return their enthusiasm. All night long, I talked and answered their questions, exhausted as I was.

Morning brought an even bigger wave of activity as the show got under way. Audience members crowded the ABC lobby, waiting to be seated inside the *LIVE!* studio. They were within sniffing distance, all asking questions simultaneously. I was on a stage where they could look up my shorts as I ran. No matter what shape you're in, or how much you've trained, you are not at your best after running twenty-four hours straight.

The filming began and Regis and Kelly came to see me. I'd covered 130 miles at the halfway point and Regis was confident I would beat the record. Kelly pointed out that the record was not the main story here. The story was about the way in which people were deeply touched by this undertaking, even driven to change their own behavior. Whether or not a record was set was inconsequential. The undertaking itself was having a huge impact. People had plastered the building with homemade signs and had written on the window with lipstick things like: "*You go, Karno!*" and "*You are an inspiration!*" and "*Never Stop!*"

Regis and Kelly eventually disappeared into their studio, and I found myself again running in the lobby without the pressure of live national television. Though the webcam still broadcasted nonstop.

I received literally hundreds of calls and text messages from

friends across the globe every time something transpired on stage—
a star appeared, a woman pressed her breasts against the glass (yes,
this really happened!), someone posted a new sign on the window,
etc. . . . The experience was dreamlike.

I began answering only calls from people whose numbers I recognized when they flashed on caller ID. When Topher called, I
knew it was only to give me grief, so I didn't take his call. I didn't
answer his second call, either. A text message arrived moments
later: "Okay, Karno, pick it up!" I realized he was watching me
check caller ID on the webcam. He could see me snubbing him over
the Internet live. How many other people, I wondered, have been
insulted while they looked on?

When guilt prompted me to accept Topher's next call, the abuse
started instantly. I put him on speakerphone, listening only intermittently. He was rambling on about how no woman ever pressed
her melons against *his* office window. Just then, Charles Gibson
walked up. One of the most respected names worldwide in news
broadcasting was now listening to my friend rambling on about a
woman smashing her breasts against a glass window.

I immediately hung up on him.

Despite overhearing Topher's childish banter, Mr. Gibson was
engaging and intelligent. He was interested in the digital panel display on the treadmill. He looked at my pace, shown in miles per
hour, and immediately calculated the equivalent "minute miles," a
staple of runnerspeak.

"You're averaging eight-minute miles," he said. "That's quite
impressive."

Surprised, I asked, "Are you a runner?" This isn't a calculation
most nonrunners would compute so quickly.

"No," he answered. "I enjoy walking, but I've never been a runner."

He mentioned something about a hopeful politician appearing on the show tomorrow, then wished me continued strength before casually breezing out. These encounters took on a cinematic quality, as though I was watching the episode on a movie screen rather than living it.

More homemade posters and messages appeared on the window, more people stopped by to run on the treadmill beside me, including friends from New York and others from across the country. How or why they were there wasn't entirely clear. Either they were out of it, or I was (in hindsight, I'm pretty sure it was the latter).

People talked to me. I nodded and smiled back as though I was with them, but I was not. I could barely process the meaning of their words. I detected their feelings—the emotions in their souls—but the dialogue seemed distracting and superfluous. It was only their spirit that interested me now. The communication was strangely deeper. I was on an acid trip of endorphins.

An Asian boy ran alongside me. I think his name is Michael, but I'm not certain. He had written me a dozen e-mails and I had seen him at many races, yet I couldn't confidently recall his name. He's a tremendous runner and terrifically dedicated and passionate about the sport, qualities I greatly admire, but he always seems awkward and uncomfortable around me, which makes me awkward and uncomfortable around him. I really liked the kid, but our communications were always disjointed and forced. The sleep-deprived haze swirling in my head made his sudden appearance seem all the more strange. I wasn't sure how or why he was here. I thought he lived in California. The more he explained it to me, the less I understood.

Finally I put my hand on his arm and said, "Let's just run." We immediately connected. No words were exchanged, we were just two men running side by side. There was something beautiful about it. We were just running, pacing off each other's movement, engaging in a celebration of perfect motion.

When he dismounted the treadmill two hours later, the moment was lost. He tried to explain something to me but the magic was gone, the conversation again awkward and strained. He sensed this and stopped talking, then mysteriously he vanished. I never saw him again.

• • • •

Now gripping pain entered the picture. Part of the problem was that the platform I was running on was not entirely stationary. The treadmill was moving slightly as I ran, and this made my muscles work harder to compensate. I asked whether anything could be done. They called a technician from the treadmill manufacturer who explained that, not only was the placement of a treadmill on a wooden platform a bad idea, but that new treadmills like this one should be recalibrated after fifty or sixty miles and the belt tightened accordingly. In other words, I was running on a wobbly treadmill with a belt that was loose, so it could possibly be recording mileage on the short side. Wonderful.

The technician lived in New Jersey. He said he could make the necessary repairs tomorrow morning, but I would be done by then one way or another.

The Guinness people didn't know anything about treadmills; they were just there to take turns standing behind me for forty-eight hours, recording the numbers that appeared on the screen. I asked the current Guinness representative if he knew the person who held the existing treadmill record. He said he'd never met him in person, but he's a professional Guinness record breaker.

"A what?" I asked. "This is what he does for a living?"

"Yes. He was on the show last year and broke the record for watching the most continuous TV. He had toothpicks propping his eyes open and we had a video camera trained on his pupils to make sure he didn't blink."

"Is he an athlete?" I asked.

"I don't think so."

"That's quite a treadmill record for a nonathlete," I said in amazement. "What's the second farthest distance anyone's covered in forty-eight hours?"

"I think it's about 190 miles, by another ultramarathoner like yourself."

"Wait a minute," I said. "You mean to tell me that this guy who's not even an athlete holds the record over an ultramarathoner by more than fifty miles?"

"I guess so," he responded.

"That must have been incredible to watch. Were you there?"

"No, I wasn't."

"Do you know where it was?"

"No, I don't. You're not actually required to have a Guinness representative present to set a record, you just need third-party verification."

I wanted to delve deeper when my phone rang.

"Hon, you need to cool off." It was Julie on the line and she could see that I was working up a sweat.

"What are you doing up so late?" I asked. It was nearly 3:00 A.M. in New York, midnight in San Francisco where she was calling from.

"I'm keeping an eye on you. It doesn't look like anyone around you is a runner."

She was right. I was overheating and the people here to support me weren't runners. I asked handler Mike, who had been sitting in a chair off to the side of me the entire time I ran, if he wouldn't mind turning the air-conditioning back on. In preparation for the show, I'd asked them to make sure there was adequate circulation and sufficient cooling. They set up two huge AC units, one behind me and one in front of me. But having the massive unit blowing icy cold, bone-dry air into my face was brutal. Imagine your car's AC blowing full blast in your face for two days straight. My sinuses and throat had become dehydrated and irritated, the frigid air overwhelming my body's natural moisturizing defenses.

"Hey, Mike," I said, trying to shift my thoughts from the AC, "have you seen that kid sitting outside on the street corner? He's been there the entire time."

"New York's full of weirdos," he said. "There's always somebody lingering. He's probably a beggar."

"I don't think so. He's just been sitting there watching me the entire time."

"We can have security ask him to leave if you want."

"No, that's all right. He seems harmless. I just think it's a little strange that some young kid would sit outside the window for two days and nights watching me, that's all."

"Like I said, New York's filled with weirdos."

People had been streaming by outside all night. Sometimes a

crowd gathered and they all started waving and chanting things. Inside the window, I couldn't hear a word. All I could see was their lips moving. When they realized I couldn't hear them, some wrote notes on paper or napkins, or typed messages on the screens of their BlackBerrys and pressed them against the window.

One guy wrote, "What kind of pizza do you like?"

I mouthed back to him, "Hawaiian-style."

Thirty minutes later, a pizza delivery guy showed up with a piping-hot Hawaiian-style pizza. It was delicious, and I began devouring it while running. Immediately, the phone rang. "Dude, that looks so tasty!" It was a friend from Australia—it was supper-time the next day down under. Even when nobody walked by on the street, those calls reminded me that I was on worldwide display.

Because I had been consuming so much liquid the past forty hours, trips to the restroom became more frequent. When I stepped off the treadmill, I no longer traveled on foot; I levitated. It felt as though I was on one of those moving walkways inside an airport terminal.

When I returned and got back on the treadmill, I noticed my shoes, socks, and lower legs were covered in black soot. Actually it was rubber dust from my feet hitting the increasingly slack treadmill deck. The belt needed to be tightened, the excess sag taken in and tensioned. My tired feet wouldn't lift high enough to clear the slight ripple in the deck being created by the increasingly flimsy belt. The minuscule abrasion this dynamic created had become exaggerated over many miles of running, fatiguing my legs further and creating a powdery black rubber dust from my shoe soles dragging across the treadmill's surface.

Even worse, with each new stride my feet slid forward in my

shoes, causing my toes to contact the front of the shoe's toe box. The cumulative effect was that some of my toenails were beginning to detach, and I was certain I would lose all ten of them eventually. Each stride on the treadmill's deck brought another jolt of pain. Eventually my feet went entirely numb.

• • • •

My dad always told me, "Son, it's not how many times you fall down that matters, it's how many times you get back up."

The problem with falling on a treadmill, however, is that you may not be able to get back up. Unlike falling on a hard surface, where you can pretty much lay motionless until you regroup, if you fall on a treadmill you are violently spit off the back. On a stationary running surface, my footing can get sloppy—as it tends to do on the second night of nonstop running—and even though I may swerve left to right, the consequences are minimal (so long as I don't get hit by a truck). But if I were to veer off the side of this treadmill, the resulting catastrophe would be spectacular. I'd be spit off the back like a sack of potatoes.

It was the bewitching hour—that transition between night and dawn that is a grunt during any multiday event—and my footing was becoming slipshod. I needed to retain razor focus to avoid falling and becoming a human projectile. I needed a power nap.

I called to Mike, but there was no response. I turned to see him slumped in his chair, sleeping. I slowly powered down the treadmill, dismounted, walked over, and tapped him on the shoulder. He opened his eyes and stared at me, then jumped up and started shaking his arms wildly, as though he'd been sitting on an anthill.

"Are you all right?" I asked him.

He took a moment to respond. "Yeah, yeah, I'm cool, I'm cool. Where are we?"

"I was hoping *you* could tell me that," I said to him. "Listen, I need to bed down for a sec."

"Huh?" He looked at me like I was from an alien planet.

"I need to lay down somewhere and get some rest."

He led me to an employee break room with a couch in it. The couch was warm and comfortable, but I couldn't sleep. I tried everything—counting down from a hundred, visualizing my bed at home, imagining myself in a deep slumber—but nothing worked. It was as if my body had adapted to running, and resting was the foreign state. Frustrated, I went back out to the fishbowl and resumed running.

Sunrise on the second day brought a new flood of activity. Crowds for the morning show assembled outside the studio. I stopped to change my shoes. Sitting on the edge of the treadmill, I felt eyeballs on me. When I turned, there were literally dozens of faces pressed against the window peering in at me. They were less than two feet away, transfixed on my every movement. I felt naked, exposed, violated. Instead of thinking of a way to shield myself, I hopped back on the treadmill and started running to get away. I didn't get very far.

Fifteen minutes went by. Then an hour. I was haggard. Also, I was chafing. A spot between my legs, where the sun don't shine, was being rubbed raw. What to do? The grating was incessant, not to mention horribly painful. A tube of Vaseline in the gear bag behind me would provide welcome relief. But here? In front of a window with now hundreds of onlookers? Could I?

Screw it. I asked Mike to hand me the tube of ointment. I dispensed a liberal gob of it in my right hand and, as discreetly as possible, reached down the backside of my shorts and massaged the soothing balm all over the problem area. Relief was instantaneous. I removed my hand and resumed a normal pace. There was nothing to wipe my hand on, so it remained gooey.

I was embarrassed to look at the crowd but a stir of commotion outside suddenly commanded my attention. I glanced over to see a procession of huge black Suburbans pulling up in front of the studio. A squadron of men wearing suits, dark glasses, and earbuds disembarked. Then, a long black limousine pulled up to the front of the building and one of the suited men opened the door. Someone exited but I couldn't tell who it was; there were too many people blocking the way. The person was ushered through the lobby, surrounded by an entourage of security agents and handlers, and taken into the ABC News studios.

Wild, I thought. But I promptly forgot about the incident and continued running.

Twenty minutes later, I noticed one of the bodyguards coming my way. What did he want with me? "There's someone here who wants to meet you," he informed me.

A posse of security guards, media escorts, advisors, and cameramen approached me. My heart started pounding faster. They were surrounding someone, maybe someone important, but I couldn't see who it was because of the encircling pack. The sea of commotion made its way over to me and the waters parted. Out from the middle of the pack stepped . . . Barack Obama.

The significance of the moment snapped me to immediate attention: The future president of the United States could be standing right next to me! I wasn't sure what to do, so I kept running. When in doubt, run, right? Only this time, like a bad dream, I wasn't getting anywhere.

Senator Obama approached the platform. "I'd just like to congratulate you," he said, and he held out his hand.

I stopped, stepped down off the treadmill, and began to extend my hand to him. What a supreme honor.

Just as we were about to clasp, I suddenly remembered the recent "lube job." Had I wiped off my hand? No, I hadn't!

The cameras were rolling. Contact was only inches away! At the last instant, I closed my hand and gave him a knuckle-clank. It was probably the wimpiest thing a man could have done—denying a handshake from the future president of the United States—but I felt it my civic duty.

He looked at me, oddly at first, perhaps unsure of the meaning of my gesture. Then he seemed to get it. He smiled broadly, closed his hand, and bumped his knuckles against mine.

We shared a few casual words and he bade me farewell, disappearing like a hermit crab back into a protective shell of bodyguards. The motorcade pulled away, and I was once again left to my running.

Outside on the sidewalk, the contingent of supporters had grown. They were chanting and screaming encouragement, though I couldn't make out a word through the glass. More signs were affixed to the window, more messages of hope and inspiration. Why this event was having such an impact on people puzzled me. Perhaps it was the raw display of human willpower. The struggling, the determination, the fight. Or perhaps it was the courage of one man to willingly put himself on public display for two solid days. Whatever the case, I needed desperately to relieve myself. Desperately.

As I prepared to dismount, the show's producer walked in. He was chatty and conversational; I was nearly comatose. "It's remarkable out there," he said. "We've never seen anything like this in the show's history. You're like Forrest Gump!"

I wasn't sure whether to feel proud or to feel like the sideshow act of a traveling circus. My mind was vacillating between the two when he continued, "After this is over, I want to talk to you about coming back on again."

Again? The thought of doing this again was about as appealing to me as contracting chicken pox a second time. "Sure, man," I shot back. "After I hop off this thing, let's jump into a group meeting. Then let's outline a preliminary action plan and start assigning duties. After that, let's get on the phone and start making calls. Oh shoot, almost forgot, I have to catch a noon flight for Europe, so we might be a little pressed for time."

That's what I *wanted* to say. Instead, I gave him the "deer in the headlights" stare. He got the message.

"Okay, we'll talk later," he said. Then he bounced off down the hallway toward the studio in his tight designer jeans.

I was happy to see him go. Being up for two nights can wear a guy thin. I mostly just wanted to be in solitude for a few hours. It is a strange sensation to be surrounded by TV cameras and hundreds of people, yet feel so isolated. Like the loneliest man on the planet. Like the *only* man on the planet. I was in so much pain, I just wanted to crawl into a hole and disappear.

• • • •

Toward the end of any extreme endurance event, you typically feel one of two ways: like Superman or like a crash test dummy. If you're not slobbering all over yourself in complete delirium, the pull of the approaching finish line can lift you through the stratosphere. Luckily, I felt the latter sensation in the lobby of ABC. I'd hit the wall a half-dozen times in the past forty-five hours, but finally I'd pushed through it and gotten another second wind. "Thou hast only to follow the wall far enough and there will be a door in it," Marguerite de Angeli once wrote.

With an hour to go, I cranked up the tempo and started banging out sub-seven-minute miles. I had scarcely covered more than two hundred miles and knew the record would not be broken. It didn't matter. I was doing the best I could—giving it my all—and that's what mattered most.

Regis commenced the countdown, "Three . . . two . . . one . . . you're finished!" The crowd cheered. The official from Guinness announced that it was a valiant effort, though in the forty-eight hours I covered only 212 miles. *Only 212 miles*. The record still stands.

"I can't believe it," Regis murmured on air. He looked distraught, stunned. Kelly quickly jumped in. "But it's really not about the record," she said spiritedly. "Just look at all those people you've inspired."

I turned to look out the window. The entire street was filled with cheering New Yorkers. She was right, the magic was undeniable. Even within the ABC studio itself—the employees, the night workers, the security guards, the group from Guinness, the newscasters, the administrative staff—people were standing around cheering. For the first time since starting this crazy endeavor, I felt mildly proud. Foolish as I'd felt most of the time treading this mill, I knew at that moment I'd done the right thing.

In all of the ensuing chaos, high-fiving, and enthusiastic pats on the back, I noticed out of the corner of my eye the kid who'd been sitting there on the street corner for the past forty-eight hours place a yellow piece of paper on the window. I thought nothing of it. There had been so many notes and signs.

The show made arrangements for me to return to the hotel for a quick shower before leaving for Europe. Yes, I really was flying transatlantic in a couple hours. I had a book signing and a marathon the next day in Portugal. Rest, right now, was a luxury I couldn't afford.

As I dashed out the studio door, gym bag filled with soiled clothes in hand, I grabbed a couple of posters and signs left outside the window as keepsakes. Flipping through them in the taxi, I came across that yellow slip of paper from the kid who had made our street corner his home for the past two days. It read: "*You are my hero. I am going to go home now. I am going to run again. Thank you.*"

I was stunned. What did he mean by "going to go home now"? Back to the Bronx to get ready for work, or back to the farm in Oklahoma to start life afresh? And "run again," what was that about? Was he a collegiate runner who had lost his way, or was he just a guy who likes to go for a jog in the morning?

These questions will go forever unanswered. But that's okay. To have motivated even one person fills me with pride. Those forty-eight hours were worth it.

As I sat in the plane high above the Atlantic, things felt surprisingly balanced. This is probably how you feel right before you die, I thought to myself. But I didn't die. I survived the flight and lived to run another day. The next, in fact, in Portugal. There ain't no rest for the weary, and that's just fine with me.

25.0

Shark Bait

"Run Silent, Run Deep."
—EDWARD L. BEACH JR.

MOST RUNNERS—including me—don't spend a lot of time worrying about drowning when they're out for a run. But that's exactly what I was thinking when I heard the hissing sound.

I was miles from shore and the thought of springing a leak hadn't even occurred to me. Until now. Worse, I noticed a swirling on the ocean's surface moments earlier and wondered what might be down there.

I wasn't equipped with a paddle, not that it mattered. This baby would sink like an anchor if it ruptured. I turned leeward toward shore and started sprinting full speed ahead.

My current predicament began in Southern California two years earlier.

"Go on . . . get in," Popou insisted. The thing looked pretty intimidating. I wasn't sure I wanted to.

We'd just spent the past half-hour pumping air into what might best be described as a massive, inflatable hamster wheel with ample space for a man to climb inside. Aside from the size, the only difference between this device and an actual hamster wheel was that the Hydro Bronc floated.

Originally designed for ice rescues on frozen lakes, the concept was that a person could propel the Hydro Bronc toward the trapped victim and if the ice were to break below, the device would float right over it. Once the stranded party was reached, the rescuer could reach down and pluck him from the frigid waters below.

It all sounded great, in theory. Just one minor issue: I wasn't on a frozen lake; I was at the beach in Southern California.

We were in the parking lot above the San Clemente Pier, the ocean churning below. Reluctantly, I climbed inside as Popou instructed, and immediately the Hydro Bronc began rolling downhill slowly at first. I began walking forward on the internal trampoline, and the contraption rapidly gained momentum. I picked up the pace, and the thing accelerated more quickly than I could have imagined. Suddenly I found myself in a literal sprint to avoid being cartwheeled inside.

The beach was up ahead and I thought for sure it would decelerate once we hit the soft sand. Nope. The Hydro Bronc now had a mind of its own. We hit the sand at full tilt and continued catapulting right across the beach. Children scurried to get out of the way, women screamed, a baby dropped his snow cone and started wailing.

The shoreline quickly approached. Surely this thing would

come to a halt once it hit the water. Hardly. It kept moving right along, and I just kept running on the internal trampoline to perpetuate the forward momentum.

Now swimmers scattered, lifeguards hollered frantic warnings, and surfers were paddling madly to get out of the way. This oversized hamster wheel was headed straight for the open ocean! Inside, running like a maniac, and hardly able to see a thing through the rotating tillers, I looked up to my left and on the pier above I spotted a group of kids running alongside me. Wait—if they were running to the end of the pier next to me, and I wasn't on the pier, then I must be running . . . on water!

Sure enough, I was doing just that. It was the oddest sensation to be running while undulating up and down as swells passed underneath. I didn't overthink things, however; I just kept putting one foot in front of the other. Soon I was out beyond the end of the pier. Now what?

Coming about in this beast took some concentration. The Hydro Bronc is largely driven by momentum, so I had to angle myself sideways as I ran; it was like running on a gyroscope. I fell over a couple times before figuring it out. After several fits and starts, I was able to spin around and face shoreward.

Proceeding toward the beach, a swell emerged behind me. As it formed into a wave, I sprinted to see if I could catch it. The peak developed and started to crest. I ran faster. Abruptly, it lifted me into the air and I began dropping down the face, the wave now fully breaking. It all happened very quickly.

I rode the swell all the way to shore, whereupon I dismounted the Hydro Bronc. I had just caught a wave while running! I'd been a runner and a surfer all my life. Never in my wildest dreams would I have imagined combining the two.

• • • •

The Hydro Bronc came up during an interview I did with *Runner's World*. The reporter was good, painstakingly so. She asked thought-provoking and insightful questions and was very thorough. Emphasis on *very* thorough. After an exhaustive three-hour Q&A session, she tossed out one final question: "So, Dean, you're kind of known as an innovative and creative guy. Working on anything crazy?"

Hmm . . . working on anything crazy? "Let's see," I scratched my head. "Well, I've been running in this device called a Hydro Bronc."

I showed her some pictures and she was intrigued. "Got any plans for it?"

"I've been considering running in one from Catalina Island to Laguna Beach."

"How far is that?"

"It's about a marathon."

"Oh, come on, Dean," she retorted. "*Just* a marathon?"

"Okay," I blurted, "from California to Hawaii!"

The story in *Runner's World* concluded by saying that I would be spending a couple months running across the Pacific.

Careful what you say to reporters.

Guess it was time to start training.

• • • •

Before setting out from San Francisco's Ocean Beach, I'd contemplated alerting the Coast Guard about my voyage but ultimately decided it would be unnecessary to do so. After all, I'd only planned a measly out-and-back 10-K. Surely the shoreline would be visible from three miles out to sea.

That was the first of my miscalculations.

The second was not wearing a life vest or other type of personal flotation device. Too wimpy, I concluded. Now that I was potentially being eyed as an afternoon snack, my attitude had abruptly changed.

Compared to the relatively friendly waters off the Southern California coast, the seas off Northern California are a bit less inviting. There are fish here. Big fish. The kind that only bite once (that's usually all it takes).

The waters off the coast of San Francisco are part of the notorious "Red Triangle," a region known to have one of the highest concentrations of great white sharks on earth (area surfers sometimes refer to great whites as the "men in white suits" or "the Governor"). Probably not the ideal place for a casual jog.

Yet here I was, miles out to sea, on a training run. The good news was that the hissing sound I heard earlier had abated. Maybe it was just the noise of some air escaping from beneath the Hydro Bronc's pontoon. Or maybe it was just my imagination. As you can imagine, I was hyperaware of anything out of the ordinary at the moment.

But wait, there it was again! Not the hissing sounds I thought I'd heard earlier, but the swirling of the ocean's surface. The churning water was, unfortunately, very real. To a man-eater, I was a ready-made meal served up on an inflatable platter. One nibble on the serving dish and I'd be instant dinner.

Panic-stricken, I watched for any telltale sign of what it could be. A moment later, my worst nightmare was confirmed. Fifteen feet in front of me, a massive dorsal fin broke the surface . . . heading straight for me. What I wouldn't give for a large spear gun. Better yet, a Coast Guard cutter with a laser-guided harpoon!

The Hydro Bronc is big, but we've all heard tales of great white sharks capsizing sturdy wooden dories in an effort to get at the occupants. There was no bright side to this situation; I was human sushi.

The fin reemerged, closing in quickly. It was a humongous slab of cartilage, jutting skyward in almost cartoonlike proportions. This had to be one of the largest sharks on record, a rogue beast worthy of main lobby display in the Museum of Natural History. I was about to be tossed into the air like a hapless beach ball and swallowed whole on the way down.

I braced for impact, but the creature swerved sideways at the last moment and passed underneath. I saw an eerily opaque eyeball staring up at me from below the surface and watched its massive midsection glide by.

But that was it. Just a giant head and body. There was no tail.

It was as though the entire hindquarters of the monster had been lopped off. Perhaps this specimen instead belonged in the Ripley's Believe It or Not! Museum in Fisherman's Wharf.

The mutant impostor made several more curious passes, freaking me out even more. It was creepy looking. From what I could tell, it looked like a giant ocean sunfish. I didn't even realize such creatures lived in these waters, but apparently they do. From my recollection of Marine Biology 101, these odd-looking fish consume principally zooplankton, not human flesh, but I wasn't sure if its presence would repel prowlers or invite company.

My heart raced. The Hydro Bronc is not the most efficient propulsion device. The rotating horizontal mainstays are less like the tillers of a paddle wheel and more like the smoothly curved pontoons of an inflatable raft. They don't scoop as much water as they turn. My adrenaline level was so high, I could have sprinted across the water faster than the Hydro Bronc was carrying me.

Going full speed, it took an anxiety-ridden hour-plus to reach shore. When I finally made it, there was no rescue party awaiting my arrival, just a few dog walkers and shell collectors who seemed only mildly interested in this strange inflatable geodesic dome that had washed up.

My hands and feet were white, wrinkled prunes. I lay in the sand on my back, contemplating how impossible it would be to propel this contraption to Catalina, let alone Hawaii. I'd been quoted in *Runner's World* saying I would do just that. Catalina, perhaps. Hawaii, no way. A man has got to know his limitations.

Don't get me wrong, running on water was fun. One of the great pleasures in life is seeking new challenges and trying different things. If I'm running, all is good, be the surface sand, snow, dirt, or, yes, even water. I'm sure some of you out there will discount the Hydro Bronc as a legitimate running device. I'll admit it's not for everyone. But it does provide a decent low-impact cardiovascular workout. And I'll guarantee you one thing: The sight of a great white closing in on you at short range will do wonders for your speed training!

► Running on water

26.0

Onward and Upward

"Poor is the pupil who does not surpass his master."
—LEONARDO DA VINCI

AFTER SUCCESSFULLY COMPLETING the Western States 100, Topher's running didn't just continue, it increased. He completed the Western States several more times in subsequent years and took on over a hundred other ultramarathons across the globe. As he scaled mountain after mountain, he also climbed the corporate ladder, quickly ascending the ranks at The North Face.

His corporate pursuits took him to Colorado, where he and Kimmy got married. I was one of his best men and Alexandria, four at the time, was their flower girl. Their new house was situated in the mountains near Aspen, and his lungs and legs developed in response to high-altitude living.

From Colorado, he accepted a position to head up The North Face Europe, and the two of them moved to a charming little town in Italy where the corporate offices were located. Topher continued to run and race, increasing his war chest of trophies and medals while simultaneously growing The North Face business at an unprecedented rate. His love of running and the outdoors was matched only by his passion for making the best gear possible for hard-core outdoor enthusiasts like himself. Topher was well liked and admired within the company, and soon he was appointed to run the entire international division. Still only in his thirties, the kid was living the dream.

I, for one, was damn glad to see it. Topher had earned every bit of his good fortune. Those same qualities that got him across the finish line of hundred-mile footraces propelled him skyward in the business world.

• • • •

Over the years, running brought Toper and me together, and it kept us together. We participated in many races and running adventures, and my family came to love Topher and Kimmy as our own. When they moved to Europe, we missed them terribly.

My life had taken some interesting turns during the course of our relationship as well. I, too, ascended the ranks of the corporate world. With dual degrees in science and business, my executive pursuits flourished.

Then something interesting happened: I wrote a book. I didn't think that many people would read it. When it became a best-seller, I was stunned. Once I got over the initial shock, I started to think that maybe there was something more here. What the heck, I figured, why not try to develop this? If not now, when? I enjoyed running itself much more than I enjoyed running a company, so I stepped away from the corporate world to pursue my passion. I could always go back to the business world, but how often does an opportunity come along to do what you actually love? One today is better than ten tomorrows.

Things went well, and I started to make a go of it. The irony, however, was that I now found myself busier than I had been in the corporate world. Happier, but busier. A garage full of belt buckles didn't keep the lights on, so I needed to find creative ways to pay the bills. Through working with my sponsors, giving corporate keynote addresses, making appearances at book signing events, writing additional manuscripts, and a plethora of other activities, I was able to cobble together a living. Keeping up with all of this was a full-time job and it sometimes left me with less available time to train.

So when Topher invited me to travel to Europe to participate in the Ultra-Trail du Mont-Blanc (UTMB)—essentially a 103-mile circumnavigation of Europe's highest peak—I jumped at the opportunity. We'd spend a week in Italy and then travel to the start of the race in France. Finally, a chance to reunite with Topher and Kim, do some running, and regain some of my training focus for a week.

Topher and Kim met me at the airport in Venice, and we spent the afternoon traveling to the lovely mountain town of Cortina in the Italian Dolomites, where they rented a small cottage and spent every available weekend.

Cortina is a beautiful town surrounded by towering mountain peaks in every direction. We decided a sunset run was in order and changed into our running gear, then off we went, bounding through the hills. Or, to state it more accurately, climbing straight up some of the most vertical inclines on the planet.

Topher and Kim were complete animals. The two of them set a breakneck pace, and it was all that I could do just to hang on their heels. They had both made running and racing an integral part of their lives, and spent countless hours training and conditioning in the mountains. It showed. Their legs were strong and their level of cardiovascular fitness was extraordinary.

"Ah . . . " Huff, puff, huff, puff. "Isn't that a ski lift?" I asked.

"Yeah, man, isn't that cool!" Topher responded, barely even breathing hard.

We kept up the insane pace. I was dying. "Ah . . . " Huff, puff, huff, puff. "Isn't that a gondola?"

"Yeah, Karno, we're heading up to Rifugio Lagazuoi," Kimmy informed me casually.

Unbeknownst to me, they were taking me to the summit of one of the most massive skiing areas in Europe.

"Isn't this pretty?" Kimmy asked.

To be honest, I could barely notice the surroundings. It was all I could do not to black out from exhaustion. They were killing me.

"Guys . . . " I said, "I've got to sit down."

I didn't just sit down, I fell down on my back in the dirt. The world was spinning.

"C'mon, Karno, we gotta keep moving," Topher told me. "Do you know what's up there?"

"Up there?" I slurred. We'd been hammering for nearly two hours and from what I could tell we were only about halfway to the summit. "Tell me what's up there, Toph. The sky? The moon? Mars? Aurora borealis?" I was convinced these two could climb to any of those distant galaxies without breaking a sweat.

"No, man, we're going to a hut."

"A hut? A hut! I'm on the verge of collapse and you're taking me to a hut?" *Oh joy*, I thought, *I'm in need of resuscitation and we're going to a dark cobblestone shed.*

"C'mon, Karno, it'll be worth it, I promise you."

Somehow, I managed to pick my weary butt off the trailside and follow them up to the "hut."

A few hours later, lounging in a warm leather recliner, glass of exquisite Italian red wine in hand, I couldn't have been more content. We'd just ordered a gourmet meal and sat around an indoor fire sipping fine vino and noshing delectably prepared hors d'oeuvres, all within the confines of this so-called "hut." The panoramic view of the city lights in the townships below was breathtaking.

"Whaddya think, Karno?"

I smirked. "Not too shabby, for a hut."

Rifugio Lagazuoi is one in a series of mountain huts principally used by hikers and climbers during multiday outings through the Dolomite mountains. Richly appointed, they are well stocked with food and supplies, and have warm showers and overnight lodging available.

This was Kimmy and Topher's training ground. They made many journeys through this pristine mountain range, running from hut to hut and using these remote outposts as restocking and refueling stations. It was the perfect setup, and the two of them took every advantage of it they could, spending endless days logging the miles along these steep and winding trails. It was no wonder they were both in such amazing shape.

I, on the other hand, had been spending too much time on the road and not enough time on the trail. The next week of training would need to be intense if I was to get myself in shape for the upcoming UTMB.

Ultra-Trail du Mont-Blanc is the preeminent off-road race in Europe. A steep and mountainous course, the route passes through three countries (France, Italy, and Switzerland). Along the way, the trail climbs and descends countless summits and valleys (basically the equivalent altitude change as the total height from sea level to summit of Mount Everest over the course of 103 miles), intersects rivers and glaciers, and has wide variations in temperature and climate. There are forests, fields of wildflowers, and open green pastures accented by dramatic rocky slopes. As far as scenery, it is an incredible natural theater. As far as difficulty, 103 miles doesn't get much tougher.

Along with the full 103-mile circumnavigation of Mont Blanc, there are two other shorter variations of the course offered. The event attracts over 3,500 participants, making it one of the largest ultramarathons on the planet.

The week of dedicated training prior to the race didn't go entirely as planned. There were marathon book signings and appearances, along with scheduled group "fun runs," all of which culminated in my hosting the grand opening celebration of the new North Face retail store in downtown Cortina. We'd managed to get some training runs in during the week, but nothing close to what I was hoping for.

When the starting gun went off, I surged forward with the rest of the pack to the best of my ability. The race was a grunt, no denying that. Many of the top European competitors utilized specially designed running poles. If you know how to use them, they can be incredibly beneficial. If you don't know how to use them, they can be incredibly hazardous to your health. Me? I don't know how to use them. However, once you decide to take the poles, the rules state that you cannot discard them and must carry them with you the entire distance. It was the first of many tactical blunders I would make during the race.

Topher, on the other hand, was quite proficient with the poles. He had trained extensively with them and had an efficient system of deploying them when necessary and attaching them to his pack when they weren't needed. He had his lighting systems dialed perfectly for the night-running segments and had strategically modified his hydration bladder to accommodate the unique demands of this particular race. He was a running machine. I, on the other hand, was a stumbling buffoon.

Nobody spoke English along the course. People were amiable and supportive, but they couldn't answer any of my questions. The food choices at the aid stations were foreign to me, too. Baguettes and soupy Gouda cheese, dried currants, hot tea—all things I wasn't used to eating. The Europeans would gobble these items by the fistful; I had a hard time stomaching any of it.

In the middle of the night, two roads diverged in the woods and I took . . . the wrong one. Topher had warned me to be cautious at this juncture, saying it was the one spot along the trail that was easy to make a wrong turn, but I still made it. Ultimately the blunder didn't matter. In fact, it only added to the race experience. I didn't go the wrong way for long, perhaps fifteen minutes, and I chuckled when I realized I'd done precisely what he'd alerted me not to do.

Overall, the race was pleasantly brutal. It was all glorious and new to me. Despite the difficulty, I was thoroughly enjoying every step. The other racers laughed at me and said things in languages I couldn't understand. They high-fived me and gave me the apple pie American thumbs-up—before dashing off down the trail and leaving me in the dust.

I kept running and running, not even sure which country I was in. I asked people along the way how much farther it was to the finish line, but nobody had any idea what I was saying. My goal was to reach the finish before the official race cutoff time, but I never knew how much farther I had to go.

Finally, at a small village late in the afternoon after running through the night, someone spoke a bit of English. I asked him how much farther it was to the finish in Chamonix. He, in turn, translated my question—in an unknown language—to one of the volunteers working at the aid station. The volunteer spoke back. Then the ad hoc interpreter answered my question: "To make the cutoff, you have twenty hours to run the next three miles." Hallelujah! Even I could manage that.

I hugged the interpreter and tried to give the volunteer at the aid station a knuckle-clank; he thought I was requesting a cup of tea. I grabbed his knuckles and gently bumped them against mine, to which all three of us started laughing and cheering.

When I reached the finish line, Topher was standing there

waiting. He was dressed in warm sweat gear, having crossed the line an hour and fifty minutes earlier, and was already partaking of his second glass of champagne (Chamonix is in France, after all).

"Karno, right on!" he yelled in his distinctly Americano accent.

"Wow," I said, "that was some good torture."

He laughed his thunderous laugh. "Can I get you anything?"

"One of those would be nice," I said, pointing to his glass of bubbly.

He chuckled and pulled the entire bottle out from his pack.

He had kicked my butt, beaten me solidly in every regard, and I couldn't have been prouder.

Here was a kid I had watched grow into a man. More deeply, here was a nonrunner I had watched grow into a champion.

"Thank you, Karno," he said to me. "Thank you for everything."

I stood there basking in the afterglow of a remarkable experience thinking just one thing: The thanks belong entirely to you, Christopher Gaylord, entirely to you.

► Training on Mont Blanc above Chamonix, France

26.2

There Is No Finish Line

"The happy traveler is not intent upon arrival."
—Tao

IT HAD BEEN SAID that the marathon doesn't really begin until mile twenty. I say mile twenty-six would be more appropriate. The final two-tenths of a mile is filled with emotion. No matter how desperately you're struggling at this point, thoughts typically drift away from the immediate task at hand (i.e., survival) to broader feelings.

For me, like other runners I've spoken with, the sight of the finish line often brings with it a sense of discontentment. It's not the finish line that matters; it's the journey, along the way.

Sure, crossing the finish line can bring with it a feeling of accomplishment, especially if you've met or surpassed any personal goal you may have set for yourself. But inevitably thoughts turn to, "What's next? Where does the road lead?"

Personally, I'm always seeking new challenges; not so much to one-up the last, but to carry forth the exploration and reward into uncharted territory. Basically, to continue the journey.

So what's next? Well, businesspeople might call it a "stretch goal," but I'll just call it a dream. I'm intending on setting a course to run a marathon in every country of the world in a one-year period. Yep, I'm planning on a global marathon expedition to visit every country on the planet in 365 days, the time it takes for our world to spin once around. Yeah, it's a colossal and bold goal, perhaps impossible, but it's still my dream, and I'm determined to make this dream come true.

There are currently 204 independent nations but there's only one world, and my desire is to have others join me along the way in a show of global solidarity. Regardless of the language one speaks, the god one worships, or the color of one's skin, we can all run together. Let's.

That's my dream. Your dream might be a little less audacious, but that doesn't matter. There's a big life out there waiting for us. Don't just stand there. RUN!

Afterword:
A Run Across America

WHEN ONE IS constantly biting off more than one can chew, he is bound to end up with indigestion at times. But this time it felt more like a case of complete gastric meltdown, the elephant I'd consumed being forcibly ejected out of all bodily orifices. My unquenchable appetite for life had caused a bit of heartburn before, but nothing life-threatening.

The morning had started with a bang, quite literally—with a fireworks show in my honor at Disneyland—but that initial excitement had ebbed and in its place was a debilitating nausea.

When Jan Schillay from the *LIVE! with Regis and Kelly* show had first contacted me regarding the possibility of running across the country, it seemed too good to be true. After all, the romantic notion of boldly striking out on foot across this great land of ours had long appealed to me. The adventures and experiences along the way would make for a lifetime's worth of memories. Jan's offer seemed a dream come true.

I should have known better. After all, this was the same woman who had once invited me to run for forty-eight hours straight, on a treadmill in NYC no less (see Chapter 24.0 for the gory details). Jan had an infectious charm about her that made not accepting her offers seem foolish, no matter how absurd those offers might be.

Still, once fooled, twice a fool. When someone whose first invitation nearly kills you proceeds to make you a second, even more outrageous, proposition, any sane individual would positively refuse the offer (in no uncertain terms). "Let's do this!" I tell her. If running shoes were gray matter, I'd be minimalist.

Now, six months later, with multimillion-dollar sponsorship commitments on the line, hundreds of people assigned to my project, and thousands of school kids across the country awaiting my arrival, I was questioning just what I had gotten myself into. More important, how was I going to get out of it?

A scant thirty-one miles into a scheduled forty-three-mile day, the heat along the roadside turned unbearable. Worse, the exhaust fumes from the busy road I was running on were nauseating. The thick, yellow-gray pollution sickened me, causing my bowels to revolt in response. But there was nowhere to go. I was stuck in the middle of this sprawling urban jungle, one that wasn't hospitable to a runner in dire straits.

Screw it, I thought, a man's got to do what a man's got to do. There was a Walgreens drugstore up ahead. Walgreens was one of the TV sponsors of the "*LIVE! with Regis and Kelly* Run Across America," so I knew they would be sympathetic to my cause. "Sir! The restrooms are for employees only!" the checkout clerk yelled at me. She wouldn't let me in.

Eventually one of my crew, the head film guy, was able to convince her to allow me access. When I discreetly exited the bathroom, the cameras were rolling. "This is going to make great TV!" he proclaimed.

The nausea worsened with each passing mile, another half-dozen episodes of intestinal upheaval occurring as I struggled to get through the end of the day. A thick, black, acidic sludge exited my mouth on the final few eruptions.

Now I found myself exhausted, lying on my back in a cold sweat, unable to sleep. The dismal hotel room I was staying in was dank and depressing. My electrolytes had been completely thrown out of balance, and I was uncertain as to whether I'd be able to get out of bed in the morning, let alone run forty-five miles. I was not sure if I should go to sleep or go to the hospital. There were literally millions of dollars riding on my ability to successfully run forty to fifty miles a day nonstop to Manhattan, yet I was a complete wreck.

The next day I still had 3,000 miles to run; that is, if I was still standing.

• • • •

Call it what you will—a death march or a survival shuffle—I downshifted into this wounded state of locomotion the mere second day of running. Until I walked into an auditorium filled with two thousand people awaiting my arrival. Time to pep up, I guess.

"Here he comes!" the announcer screamed over the loudspeaker. Haggard and staggering, operating on four hours of sleep, it was time to speak cogently and intelligently. I approached the microphone, "Um . . . does anybody have a couch I could crash on?" They all laughed. They must have thought I was kidding.

• • • •

Much of the Run Across America unfolded in this disjointed, dreamlike manner. Hopefulness could become hopelessness in a single stride. No downtime was scheduled. Public appearances popped up suddenly, followed by twelve-hour continuous runs which seemed to drag on endlessly. Celebration with a crowd could spontaneously devolve into survivalism on the open road. Conversely, road-weary desperation could blossom into energized inspiration just as swiftly.

• • • •

After a week of running, I approached Albuquerque and saw a group of women standing up ahead on the roadside. They were holding signs and wielding cameras with posters at the ready. People had been stopping me along the way for pictures and autographs, more frequently as the trip progressed, to the point that it was slowing me down considerably. I was running with one of my crewmembers who was expert at shielding me from the fanfare.

"There he is!" they squealed as I got closer. I braced myself for the mobbing.

"Oh Harald . . ." they cooed. "Can we PLEEEASE have your autograph?"

A humbling reality check. I smiled and nodded at Harald, my main crewmember, who would spend all seventy-five days by my side. Broad shouldered and tanned with mesmerizing blue eyes, Harald is a trained killer. Literally. An esteemed member of the elite Navy SEALs Special Ops forces, he is the best in the business.

Harald posed graciously for some photos, his demeanor humble and unassuming. A small crowd gathered, and he kept a cool watch over the assemblage. Should any signs of trouble emerge Harald could efficiently dispatch the threat and resume signing autographs without a single lock of his flowing, sun-bleached hair out of place. Then he could run thirty miles by my side without breaking a sweat.

My team consisted of athletes, trainers, a nutritionist, logistics specialists, event managers, and media liaisons. I was accompanied by some of the leading experts in the industry, many of whom I had handpicked myself. However, I inherited the ABC film crew. All of them were from New York and they were high strung and hurried. There were personality clashes and power struggles. Watching their drama unfold was like watching a spirited episode of *Keeping Up with the Kardashians*. There were times when my team felt certain they would kill each other before reaching the far side of the country.

What happened along the way surprised us instead. They started running! The more road miles that they logged with me the more harmonious things became, this despite the head TV director continuing to wear his tight designer jeans and black leather vest throughout our travels across rural midwestern farmlands. The

Amish residents thought we were weird, running down their cornfield-lined roads in brightly colored running gear, until they got a load of Jonathan screaming director's cues through a megaphone. Then they thought we were from Mars.

• • • •

LIVE! organized a dozen or so 5-Ks for me to run as I made my way across the country. Many were simple runs at local schools; others were quite elaborate, like the first group in history to run a lap around the famed Indianapolis Motor Speedway. Hundreds, sometimes thousands, of other runners joined me, as well as a cadre of local dignitaries and government officials. One of the runs even finished on the South Lawn of the White House, where First Lady Michelle Obama greeted us and served snacks to the children who ran with me.

These organized 5-K events were a terrific forum for me to interact with other runners, both young and old, and we raised nearly $200,000 for Action for Healthy Kids. This was all a wonderful addition to the endeavor.

Or a horrible distraction, depending on your point of view. The 5-K mileage was not calculated into the total distance of the cross-country run and it took precious time away from my primary goal of successfully running to NYC. While participating in these 5-Ks I often found myself anxious and restless, knowing that I still had forty or fifty miles of road left to cover.

Often this led to conflicted feelings of guilt—trying to reconcile my desire to connect with runners and kids at these 5-Ks with my burning impulse to get the heck out of there as quickly as possible so that I could knock out my obligatory forty or fifty miles for that day.

It weighed heavily on me emotionally, until a little boy in Wichita reminded me of something. "Mr. Karnazes," he said, "I run because of you. You're the luckiest person I know." From that day forward I would spend all day at these events even if it meant I would have to run straight through the night. He reminded me of just how lucky I really was.

• • • •

We are told that America is a culturally rich and geographically diverse land. I had the good fortune of experiencing it all firsthand, along with developing the uncanny ability to detect which fast-food chains maintain the cleanest restrooms.

There were stunning and dramatic landscapes along the way, like Salt River Canyon in Arizona, and there were crime-filled backstreets, like East St. Louis. This country is a land with striking contradictions and juxtapositions, some of them not so good, others really quite mysterious and wonderful.

Take the Quartzsite Yacht Club, for instance, where we were invited to spend the night carte blanche at their opulent bayside marina. They threw a celebration on our behalf. The local sailors came to see the captain of the guild bestow upon us honorary life membership in the club. Something seemed strangely amiss, though. The motto of the Quartzsite Yacht Club is, "Long Time, No Sea." The motto makes sense: Quartzsite is in the middle of the Arizonian desert, where there hasn't been water in a million years! My lead trainer and coach, Jason Koop, pointed out that Quartzsite wasn't all too far from Area 51. Time to sail off into the distance. Quickly. Legs, don't fail me now!

At a later point in the journey we stumbled upon Pie Town. You might imagine this to be located in a municipality near Delaware or in an area where little pastry shops abound. Pie Town, population 75, is situated in the outer reaches of New Mexico, surrounded by miles of cactuses and tumbleweeds. But don't let that fool you. They make some of the freshest fruit pies on earth! I think the entire town works at the pie factory, and they are complete masters of their craft. The staff treated us to a half-dozen hot-out-of-the-oven pies. Those babies lasted all of about fourteen milliseconds before being voraciously devoured. I nearly lost a finger or two trying to get my fair share.

Crossing the border into Texas, we were enlivened by a billboard that had been posted by a local employment agency. It advertised:

> *Not all jobs have been*
> *Outsourced*
> *Necesita un empleo?*

Farther down the road passing through the Hillbilly County of the Ozark Mountains, the discharge of rifle shots periodically cracked through the valleys, and I noticed a small, hand-painted roadside placard. Ozark moonshine whiskey is legendary in these parts. So too, I quickly learned, is the hospitality extended to strangers. The sign welcomed individuals to enter the kingdom of the Lord, though it offered a slightly less encouraging invitation to enter their own personal roadside kingdom. It advised:

Prayer is the best way to meet God.
Trespassing on my property is a faster way.

Needless to say, I chose not to venture down that particular driveway to relieve myself.

On a warm and dry afternoon while running though the pastoral countryside of rural Ohio, I heard a frail old voice calling to me: "Oh, there you are, sonny! I've been waiting for you all day."

I turned to see an elderly woman sitting in a rocking chair on the porch of an old-fashioned white house. "Come on up here," she summoned.

I made my way through the rustic white picket fence, up the wooden stairs, and onto the front porch. It was as though I had just entered a Norman Rockwell painting.

"Put your face right down next to mine," she requested politely.

This sweet old lady is lonely, I'm thinking to myself, she just wants to touch cheeks together or something. I lower my face next to hers.

She whips an iPhone out of her pocket, holds it up in front of us, and commands, "Smile!" She quickly snaps a shot and giggles in delight, "I can't wait to post this on my Facebook page, all my friends are going to be so jealous!"

• • • •

Upbeat and fun as some of these stories may sound, there wasn't anything particularly easy about running 3,000 miles. Layer the physical challenges of running such immense distances on top of the mandatory TV appearances, sponsorship obligations, and 5-K events, and I felt at times as though every single cell in my body was completely tapped out.

• • • •

The difficulties began early on as asphalt temperatures crossing Arizona's desert rose to more than 100 degrees. None of us had anticipated it would be so hot this early in the year. After all, it was still wintertime.

Then I faced the Continental Divide, where breathing the thin mountain air was arduous. Living at sea level I don't have an opportunity to do much altitude training, and the elevation crushed me.

We were assured that the terrain would flatten once we reached the Midwest, and that we would be buffeted by a consistent tailwind that blew reliably from west to east across the Great Plains. Arriving in Kansas, we were greeted by a late-season blizzard accompanied by freezing cold temperatures and a predominate headwind blowing from east to west. The sleeting wet snowfall made keeping dry impossible. No matter how much technical raingear you layered on, the wind drove the cold wet right through every tiny crevice in the fabric.

When the cold snap ended, it was almost immediately replaced by oppressive humidity in Missouri. Temperatures crept into the 90s, the air becoming thick and stagnant. We tried to avoid the busy interstate highways, which meant that the routes I traveled were hilly and less graded than the main thoroughfares. The abrupt climbs and rapid descents continued all the way until we crested the Appalachian Trail in Pennsylvania, some 2,700 miles from the start.

The demanding terrain and extremes in weather only tell part of the story. Breathing polluted air from vehicle exhaust all day while running through congested metropolitan sections of the country added quite an unpleasant element to the challenge. Even more disturbing was the noise pollution created by these massive 18-wheel semi-trailer trucks whizzing by just feet—sometimes inches—away from me. Some days I endured this terrifying onslaught for upwards of ten straight hours.

Watching my life flash before my eyes multiple times throughout the day grew a bit unnerving. Twitching in my bed from nightmares of being run down, some nights I found it difficult to sleep. Once I couldn't sleep at all, so I got up and ran. That day I covered 78 miles.

• • • •

Fifty-three pairs of destroyed shoes and three lost toenails later, I arrived in NYC a fundamentally different person than the one who had departed from California two and a half months earlier. You learn a lot about yourself during such an undertaking. You adapt, you grow. You overcome demons and self-doubt. After all, the real battle is within.

Some of what I learned about myself I liked; other elements I didn't. My crew was out there every single day starting at four in the morning busting their butts to support me, yet sometimes I reacted sharply and ungraciously toward them—the equivalent of biting the hand that feeds—and while I knew this was wrong, I couldn't seem to control myself. There were times that I was hanging on by a mere thread and was in so much pain that I just wanted it all to end, someway, somehow. Nothing they did at these points was enough, though there was nothing more they really could do. On several occasions I found myself apologizing for my demanding and unpredictable behavior. It was a character weakness of my own and no fault of theirs.

I learned that I possess an unwavering discipline when striving to achieve a lofty goal. For seventy-five straight days I ate the exact same bland foods. Once I found a dietary formula that worked, I took no chances and didn't permit myself a single indulgence. After a while you'd think it'd seem dull, but it became what I needed to do to make it and the more difficult things got, the more tenacious my determination grew to succeed.

I learned that one could overcome mind-numbing boredom, contend with untold adversity, and push through tremendous pain and insecurity simply by being present. Instead of repeating a mantra or searching for some diversionary tactic when the pain set in, I would instead confront it head on. I would focus on the pain, dissect the root of its cause, and attempt to explain why pain is pain. I would live entirely in the moment, focusing completely on the here and now, just taking every next step to the best of my ability. There was no future preoccupying my thoughts, and no past reflections consuming my attention. There was only the mission of putting one foot in front of the other over and over again. How do you run across America? Simple, one step at a time.

The Run Across America taught me that there are no shortcuts or paths of least resistance on the road to reaching something worthwhile. In times of struggle you inevitably turn inward, and when you do you will either say to yourself: "I paid my dues. I didn't skimp in my training or preparation. I always went the extra mile," or you will say to yourself: "I cut my training short. I didn't do all that I should have. I gave it less than my best effort." The secrets for success are really no secrets at all: hard work, dedication, commitment, and sacrifice. Anything short of that is a compromise, and you're only cheating yourself.

I also learned that passion and conviction are more important than talent, the former of which I have in overabundance, the latter of which I have almost none. Find that which you truly love and pursue it with heartfelt fervor. You will realize an inner strength that is boundless and an external energy that is indefatigable. The Portuguese have a telling proverb: *Quem corre por gosto, não cansa* (who runs for pleasure never tires). Do what you love. Dream big. Be restless. Sleep little. Don't play life safe; dare boldly instead. Live as though you really mean it.

Finally, I learned that if you keep tirelessly chasing your dreams, one day you just might catch one. You don't always have to go fast, you just have to go. I'd always dreamed of running across America, and the fact that I was able to meet some great folks along the way and perhaps influence a few of them to become more active made the venture all the more exceptional. It took 3,000 miles to realize this dream, but it was worth every step of the way.

We runners are a unique breed. We like chasing dreams. We are kindred spirits in this regard. Whether your dream is running across America, tackling a marathon, or completing your first 5-K, it really doesn't matter. When you distill it all, we don't run for the trophies or the records or the recognition, we run because a rapidly beating heart pumps more life through our veins.

Our ultimate calling is not to arrive at the finish line in a composed state, but rather to stagger in breathlessly, totally annihilated and on the verge of collapse, proudly knowing in our hearts that we have run our race, and it was glorious. Whether you end up with a medal being placed around your neck or an IV line being placed into your arm, the inner bliss is the same. You have waged your war and you have emerged victorious. You are content. If you are never to take another step, you will forever remain satisfied. The job is done.

That is, until the next one. Yeah, every runner knows the feeling.

Cool Down

WHERE TO START? How to possibly acknowledge all those people who have provided the foundation for this book? Let me start in the beginning, with my mom. Mom, thank you for putting me in a stroller and pushing me around town from sunup till sundown since the day I was born. You were my first partner in adventure, and even though I couldn't voice my opinion (hey, I was only an infant at the time), I loved every second of it!

To my wonderful and supportive family, I only wish there was some way I could reciprocate the love and understanding you have shown me. I am deeply appreciative of the freedom and latitude you have always afforded me without ever making me feel guilty or neglectful. I haven't necessarily been there for every ballgame, school dance, or office party, but you have always welcomed me home with open arms and affection. Please know that you mean the world to me and that nothing I have done, or endeavor to do, would ever be the same without you. You are, and will forever be, my first love.

To Topher and Kim, and indeed the entire Gaylord clan, thank you for showing me what true friendship is all about. It's been a wonderful journey, and it keeps getting better and better as the years roll by.

To the folks at Rodale: David Willey, Bart Yasso, Mark Remy, John Atwood, and especially my editor, Shannon Welch, thanks for believing in me as much as I believe in you.

To Coach Harwood (writing coach, that is), your patience, subtle guidance, and delicate tutoring during the equivalent of teaching an elephant to tap dance was commendable. Writing doesn't come easy to me, but you were a skilled mentor every step of the way.

I'd like to thank my agent, Carole Bidnick, for tirelessly supporting my far-flung proposals and far-off wanderings. Over the years, you have demonstrated incredible endurance and stamina. I know there's a runner in there somewhere!

Special thanks to Jan Schillay of the *Live! with Regis and Kelly* show for making running on a treadmill for forty-eight hours about as pleasant as, well, running for forty-eight hours on a treadmill possibly could be and for more recently getting me safely across the country. I shudder to think what's next, and I look forward to it!

Finally, I owe a marathon of gratitude to my friends, sponsors, and supporters. In so many ways, we're all in this together. Let me propose something to you: I'll keep going, if you keep going. Deal? (Think I already know the answer; that's why I love ya all!)

About the Author

DEAN KARNAZES, athlete and bestselling author, was named by *Time* magazine as one of the Top 100 Most Influential People in the World. A passionate advocate for healthy, active living, Dean has been so well received not because he runs hundreds of miles, but because he inspires others to be the best that they can be.

A lover of adventure, Dean has pushed his body and mind to inconceivable limits. Among his many accomplishments, he's run 135 miles nonstop across Death Valley in 120-degree temperatures and a marathon to the South Pole in minus 40 degrees. On ten separate occasions, he's run a two-hundred-mile relay solo, racing alongside teams of twelve.

Dean is the winner of the Vermont 100 Endurance Race, the Badwater Ultramarathon, the 4 Deserts Race Series, and holds eleven Western States 100-Mile Endurance Run Silver Buckles. He's run 50 marathons in 50 states in 50 consecutive days and recently ran across America from California to NYC. He's an ESPN ESPY award winner, one of *Outside* magazine's Top 10 Ultimate Athletes, and a member of the *Men's Journal* Adventure Hall of Fame.

His incredible endeavors have been featured on *60 Minutes*, the *Today* show, the *Late Show with David Letterman*, *Late Night with Conan O'Brien*, the *Howard Stern Show*, NPR's *Morning Edition*, CNN, BBC, and many other media. He has appeared on the covers of a dozen magazines and been featured in *Time*, *Newsweek*, *People*, *GQ*, *Runner's World*, *Esquire*, *Forbes*, the *New York Times*, *USA Today*, the *Washington Post*, *Forbes*, and the London *Telegraph*, to name a few.

Beyond being an acclaimed endurance athlete, philanthropist, public speaker, and bestselling author, Dean is an accomplished businessman with a notable professional career working for Fortune 500 companies and start-ups alike. He has worked tirelessly to raise millions of dollars for charities across the globe.

Dean lives with his wife and family in the San Francisco Bay Area.

For more information, visit www.ultramarathonman.com
and facebook.com/ultramarathon.